TOUCHING TOMORROW

TOUCHING TOMORROW

Coming of Age in Post-War Cornwall

by

ELSIE BALME

Kirrier-Porthleven

First published in 2004
Kirrier-Porthleven, Dai-Mar, Fore Street,
Porthleven, Cornwall TR13 9HH

Copyright © Elsie Balme 2004

ISBN 0-9532292-8-9

Cover photography by André Ellis

Printed by Intype London Ltd,
Unit 3 & 4 Elm Grove Industrial Estate, Elm Grove, Wimbledon,
London SW19 4HE

Available from Elsie Balme,
6 Sunset Gardens, Porthleven, Cornwall TR13 9BS

ACKNOWLEDGEMENTS

Cover design

Bill Scolding
Serpentine Design
Cadgwith
Helston TR12 7JZ

Photoediting

Amanda Auguste

Other photographs
kindly supplied by

Mrs Sheila Richards
Mr David Benney
Mrs Rosemary Polglase

Gala Week programme
kindly supplied by

Mr John Strike

Editor

Gill Oxford

Typesetting

Barbara Tucker

LIST OF ILLUSTRATIONS

Frontispiece Under the Cherry Tree in 1946

Between pages 80 and 81

Official Gala Week programme, 1947
Schedule for the 1947 Carnival

Frontispiece: Under the Cherry Tree in 1946

CONTENTS

PROLOGUE

"Under the Cherry Tree"

HELSTON Flora Day, 1946, falling as it did precisely one year to the day after the end of the war in Europe, was a celebration conducted against a background of continuing austerity, shortages and rationing. It was nonetheless a great occasion, to which people flocked from far and wide, determined to derive the maximum enjoyment out of the proceedings. It is important to remember that "peacetime" was still very much a novelty to our generation. We had grown accustomed both to the hardships and deprivations of war and to apprehension over the safety of loved ones in the Armed Forces. Many of these latter had by now been "de-mobbed" and were at home enjoying their own first tastes of Flora Day for the best part of seven long years; hence the prevailing atmosphere of jubilation and delight.

It must be admitted, however, that one obvious consequence of the war's aftermath was a certain dearth of glamour, with few new dresses to be seen. "Make-do-and-Mend" was still very much the order of the day. I wore a quite respectable hand-me-down from an older

1

friend; photographs of the occasion show that it was somewhat too wide in the shoulders and far too full in the chest, so that it hung limp as a dying snowdrop on my skinny young frame. But it was white; it was crepe de chine; carefully washed and pressed it seemed as good as new: nothing else mattered. I felt like a princess, wearing it to dance the Flora for the very first time at the age of twelve.

There is a great deal of available verbiage about Flora Day, much of which tends to be fulsome and over-stated. Indeed, the local press experience an annual shortage of superlatives as they vie with one another to encapsulate the charm and allure of the occasion. The day is not, however, without its critics, who contend that in recent years the whole event has become over-orchestrated and lacks spontaneity. The truth probably lies somewhere between the two extremes: certainly when I was twelve years old it was a day of complete enchantment. I have taken part in the occasion many times since, including a couple of appearances in the prestigious mid-day dance; the pleasure did not even begin to compare with the delights of that first May morning long ago, when the war was over and we were touching, as it were, a bright tomorrow, full of promise and fulfilment.

My somewhat reluctant partner for the occasion was a boy called Michael Jewell, a Porthlevener like myself, on whom I had an on-going crush. I had shamelessly asked him to dance with me and he had accepted, though whether because he was embarrassed to refuse or because I was a useful batting partner at cricket on summer evenings, I never did discover! Enough for me at the time that I had secured a male partner: girls always outnumbered boys in the children's dance and often had to partner each other, thus rendering themselves objects of pity to the more fortunate.

Images of that first Flora Day, and indeed of those which followed throughout my Helston schooldays, remain firmly fixed in the mind, merging to provide a mental montage of joyful sunlit mornings, full of innocent pleasure. Like many of life's pleasures, however, the anticipation equalled – perhaps almost exceeded – the delights of the event itself. Even the rehearsals round and round the school hall on wet Wednesday afternoons under the eagle eye of the Games Mistress provided a frisson of excitement and a welcome break from the perceived tedium of lessons.

The day itself was always the re-enactment of the time honoured ritual. You assembled in the school yard of the old Grammar School in Penrose Road - though the yard itself (now a car park) fronted Wendron Street. The atmosphere was akin to that of a large beehive, full of comings and goings and buzzings. Here were hundreds of white-clad children of all ages getting in each other's way: small scuffles occasionally breaking out between boys: girls fussing with one another's hair and anxious mothers who ought not to have been there at all trying to persuade their offspring to keep their cardigans on until the very last minute.

The final line-up would be chaotic: someone from one set of four or another would always have gone down the night before with chicken-pox or mumps, necessitating frantic last-minute re-groupings. Someone would arrive late, their bus having broken down on the way in from Manaccan or Ruan Minor or Four Lanes, and inevitably someone would discover a desperate need to go to the toilet at the very last minute, just as the band were about to strike up.

Meanwhile the bandsmen themselves would lounge around Wendron Street, unscrewing the mouthpieces of their instruments to blow out the accumulated saliva from the Seven o'clock dance; the sweet smelling lily of the valley in their hats already starting to go limp; their collars temporarily loosened in a vain attempt to keep cool in the mounting heat. Having already marched around Helston once in the cool of the early morning they would do so three times more before their day was over, blowing without much respite and incurring very sore mouths. Their ages varied. Elderly men and schoolboys marched side by side – I do not remember any girls in the band at that time. Their pride was the tune; simple, catchy, yet somehow never quite caught by any other group of musicians. It was Helston's tune, just as it was Helston's day, even though some of us from the surrounding villages were generously suffered to take part in it.

Teachers from the various Helston schools always accompanied the children's dance, as indeed they still do. This is a very wise precaution, as minor disasters tend to occur. As we danced up Meneage Street in 1946, Michael had his shoe wrenched off by the heavy foot of an over-enthusiastic Denton Webb from Form 1B, dancing too close behind him. Needless to say, the shoe laces went into a tight knot, and the good offices of the female teacher accompanying our section of the dance were needed to untie it and restore the shoe. Meanwhile I danced on, partnerless but happy, although somewhat confused, as most of us were, by the fact that the front section of the band, coming back down Meneage Street, were playing the opening bars of the tune "Te tum, te tum, te tum tum tum.." whilst the second section, still leading the rear of the dance up the street, were playing the later passage "Tiddly-um tum tum tiddle iddle tum tum..." etc.

The offending shoe restored to its owner's foot, and the disconcerting anomaly in the music being sorted out by the departure of the leading band down round the corner into Church Street and out of earshot, we danced

4

on as though our lives depended on it, arriving with not a little relief at the halfway stopping point in Lismore Gardens, where bandsmen drank beer and families camped out on the grass with rugs and thermos flasks, and if you were lucky someone might offer you a drink of lemonade.

Lismore Gardens really need a special mention - they were, perhaps, the pivotal point of Flora Day. Home of a local doctor, who took pride in opening them to the public for Helston's great occasion, they made the perfect setting for a perfect day, with their manicured, sloping lawns flanked by beds of late spring flowers and a small lake at the lower end where you danced along a cool, shady, tree-lined path and ducks splashed excitedly in the water as the band marched by.

The pièce de resistance, however, was the magnificent cherry tree "Prunus Hisakura" which stood sentinel in the midst of the garden. Covered in masses of blowsy pink blossom, it had usually begun by Flora Day to shed its petals, which would fall in great drifts around your head as you posed self-consciously under the tree whilst your mother manoeuvred her Box Brownie to record the great occasion for posterity. The whole thing held, for me at any rate, an aura of glamour thitherto only experienced at second-hand in romantic films.

Flora Day, however, was better than any film. It was live theatre and you were a star.

CHAPTER 1

Latin and Logarithms

THE realities of everyday life in 1946 were far removed from the romantic settings of Flora Day. Life was, nonetheless, challenging, exciting and, if truth is told, just a little intimidating at times. In September 1945 I had moved from Porthleven County Primary School to Helston Grammar, an honour shared with five of my contemporaries, including my erstwhile Flora Day partner. We had all "passed the scholarship"(the phrase "eleven-plus" was yet to be coined) and were deemed by the fairly exacting standards of the age bright enough to embark upon academic careers in the select confines of the Grammar School, an institution with long traditions in Helston, with such luminaries as Charles Kingsley claimed amongst its "old boys".

We lived, however, not in Helston, but in Porthleven, where "Passing the scholarship" was no passport to popularity and certainly set you upon no pedestal of public esteem: quite the reverse in fact. Your peer group who remained behind in the Porthleven schools immediately set themselves the task of cutting you down to size, and in many cases took a fiendish delight in taunting you with rude catcalls and insulting you with nicknames such as "Grammarsow" (a local dialect word for a woodlouse!). You were invariably accused of snobbery, and might well find yourself ostracised by people who were formerly your friends. When you are only eleven years old, this sort of thing can be most perplexing and not a little painful. My own way of dealing with it was to drop my aitches as I stepped off the school bus, and revert to as broad a dialect as, given my upbringing by a non-Cornish mother, I was capable of affecting. The aim of this rather odd behaviour was to reassure my contemporaries that I was still me, and had not been transmogrified into some haughty and unapproachable being, who thought herself better than she really was. It seemed, for the most part, to work, and I was not greatly persecuted in the village in consequence of my elevation to higher education, though some of my contemporaries remained wary and sceptical.

This strange disapproval of the Grammar School even surfaced amongst grown-ups, some of whom, at least in the circles in which my parents moved, still held to the somewhat outmoded belief that education for girls was a complete waste of time because they would marry at twenty and spend the rest of their lives bringing up children. Happily such people were already in a minority in September 1945, and I derived a great deal of encouragement from local adults who urged me to make the best of my chances of a decent education.

To achieve this it was necessary largely to forego Thursday night sprees to the pictures in the Public Hall and buckle down instead to unaccustomed levels of homework. Much of this was on subjects which were thitherto unexplored territory, and required varying degrees of effort in order to get to grips with them. Some of it I found easy and delightful; French, for instance, presented me with no problems at all. Algebra and, more particularly, geometry, I thoroughly detested. My difficulties with the latter were compounded by the continuing lack of manual dexterity which had dogged my childhood: one maths teacher, who shall remain nameless, observed my struggles with the compasses and compared me, unkindly, I thought, to "a cow handing a musket"!

At that early stage in our academic careers, we went in awe of certain teachers, notably one J.A. Shimmin, the school's senior master , who taught history. A Manxman, a confirmed bachelor, and a truly terrifying disciplinarian, he was as bald as an egg, and had a severe astigmatism in one of his eyes, so that you were never quite sure in which direction he was looking; indeed he seemed to have the ability to be looking everywhere at once, particularly if you were doing something you ought not to have been doing. "Shimmy" as he was known, was renowned especially for awarding quarters of a mark - five marks and you were safe for a day or two - four and three quarters, however, would necessitate a rather uncomfortable visit to his office during the lunch break to receive a dressing-down and instructions to re-write the offending piece by the next day. I once got ten marks from Shimmy for a history essay; it was an unrepeatable feat: on another occasion I got nine and three quarters - he had deducted a quarter of a mark for a minute error in punctuation. Shimmy got on better with seniors than he did with juniors - he would admit that he was not over-fond of young children, though he told us, during our second year, that we were "not a bad bunch". My own relationship with him was complicated by the fact that my father, who drove a taxi at weekends, often collected Shimmy from his home in Helston to transport him to church in Porthleven. A high Anglican, he much preferred the elaborate ceremonial of worship at St. Bartholomew's to the simpler rituals of St. Michael's in

Helston. During those taxi rides my academic prowess apparently came under discussion, and I would squirm with embarrassment when I next saw Shimmy, remembering the things my father maintained to have been said, though he was a dreadful tease and I imagine that a great deal of the alleged conversation was invented for my benefit!

Long afterwards, when he finally retired from teaching, it was my privilege to be chosen to write an appreciation of Shimmy on behalf of all his old pupils - thousands of us, over the years. My remarks then - published in the old "Helstonian" magazine, might have seemed fulsome to the casual reader who had not known the man very well. For my part I stand by them. Shimmy was a great teacher and an exceptional man: in a world of duplicates and copies he stood out as an original.

This is not to imply that the rest of the staff lacked character. Maybe the shades of all schoolteachers tend to assume proportions of personality that they never, in real life, possessed, but I do not think it is a conceit to claim that Helston Grammar in our time was particularly well-endowed in that respect. There was, for instance, Les Blewett - Senior Maths and Gardening. This latter derived from the need to "Dig for Victory" during the war, when he had dragooned a group of senior boys into horticulture, whether they would or no, and vast quantities of vegetables were produced on a piece of land behind the gym. The war ended, but the gardening went on, at least in my time at the school. Mr. Blewett was an avid gardener, his love of digging in the earth seemingly only equalled by his love of mathematics! A square man, with a square head, you wondered whether it would be possible to discover his square root! He was, however, a being of considerable charm, in spite of - or perhaps even because of - a small but pronounced stutter. "It isn't ccccan't, old soul, it's wwwwon't" he would declare benignly when you had got something wrong for the third or fourth time. Once, totally exasperated by my own incompetence, I proclaimed angrily "Can't, won't and shan't". Unphased by this outburst, he subsequently addressed me as "Can't won't and shan't" on every possible occasion, beaming triumphantly as he did so.

Then there was R.J. "Johnny" Holden (Physics and Sports). To put it as delicately as possible, he did not seem entirely built for sports when I knew him, but he often still refereed at football or cricket and seemed to greatly enjoy that side of his work. He never taught me: girls were discouraged from studying physics, and I needed little such discouragement, the subject being totally alien to my capacities. Those who were taught by Johnny went in some awe of him: it was whispered that on occasions he had been known to twist boys' ears! He was also a very fine baritone singer. We had a tradition of end-of-term in-house concerts, at which the staff let their hair down and performed in front of the pupils; "Johnny" was always called upon to sing on these occasions - usually some favourite from Gilbert and Sullivan, though I well remember a fine performance of "Mamma's little baby loves shortening bread" which practically brought the house down.

One of Johnny's most popular renditions, however, was "A Bachelor Gay", the word "gay" in those days carrying its original and unadulterated meaning of "happy" or "light-hearted". Johnny was certainly viewed as a confirmed bachelor. It caused quite a stir, therefore, when during our third year he married Miss Howard (French, Maths and Music). We clubbed together to give them a Qualcast lawn-mower, which was proudly presented on stage in the Hall after morning prayers, the headmaster making a somewhat coy speech to mark the occasion.

Our headmaster was a cricket-loving Yorkshireman, named H.E. Stanley Dransfield. I never learned what the H. and E. stood for; he was known somewhat disrespectfully, as "Dranny". He taught Latin, and tended to be somewhat obsessed with the importance of the subject. This had given rise to the following rhyme, which became one of the sillier parts of the school's folklore:-

Drannibus satibus on the deskolorum,
Deskibus collapsibus – Dranny on the florum.

I think it is only fair to say of Dranny that, whatever his shortcomings, he looked the part of a headmaster, carrying his tall if somewhat portly frame almost regally round the corridors and sweeping majestically into the hall wearing his mortar board to take morning assembly. He was proud of his school and liked to be regarded as a father figure within it. He was always particularly delighted to announce the winning of a football or cricket match: when we had lost, he would excuse the team by pointing out that the larger school against which we had played "had so many more boys to choose from". Dranny retained more than a touch of his native speech, which was no bad thing in itself, but I recall an occasion when it let him down rather badly in front of the whole school. On the morning of Speech Day, it was customary for us to rehearse the school hymn during assembly. The said hymn was "Land of our Birth", the last line of which read "Head, heart and hands in the years to be". The hymn was duly sung. Dranny expressed himself not entirely pleased with the performance. Some of us had dropped our aitches in the last line, and this would not do. "You mustn't sing 'ead, 'eart and 'and" he proclaimed – "you must sing **H**ead, **H**eart and **H**and. Now let us pray. Lord, we give Thee our 'umble and 'earty thanks ..." To our credit, no-one actually laughed out loud, though whether this was from good manners or fear of reprisals I shall never know.

A famous character, not just in the school but in the entire neighbourhood, was the woodwork master, one Walter Quick: he was well-known, amongst other things, for hurling off-cuts of wood (and sometimes even the odd chisel) across the room at recalcitrant boys, some of whom came in from the country schools once a week to be instructed in his craft. It was rumoured that he drank a great deal; nonetheless he enjoyed considerable popularity in the area.

Just as boys came in to do woodwork, girls descended on us from all points of the compass on certain days for cookery classes, the village schools lacking all facilities for that sort of thing. There were times when I wished we lacked them as well; this would have obviated the need for doing cookery, always a high-risk occupation for me in those days. I frequently under-cooked, or burned, or otherwise spoiled the dish I was supposed to be preparing and would be scolded by Miss Slade or her successor, Miss Williams for having wasted scarce and precious ingredients. I have to say in my own defence that this was not always my own fault: what is one supposed to do when, having put into the oven something needing long, slow cooking, that same oven is seized upon by another person, who turns the heat up for her own nefarious purposes, thus blackening not only the recipe, but one's own fragile reputation as a cook? Small wonder that I never learned to enjoy cooking until long after I had left school.

There were compensations, however, for the drudgery and humiliation of cookery classes. The dry store cupboard in the domestic science room was a walk-in affair and once inside you were away from the eagle eye of the teacher. Most of what was stored there was, it must be admitted, very dull stuff; lentils, dried peas;

macaroni; semolina.....but on the end shelf, farthest away from the door, were some fairly large containers of dried fruit, in particular a fine jar of raisins. I loved raisins, my taste for which had been somewhat frustrated by rationing. So it was that during a particularly disastrous cookery lesson I strayed into the cupboard and found myself eyeing the raisins. In my own defence I must record that I was never a natural thief: temptation overcame me, however, on this occasion. How easy to remove the lid, grab a handful and enjoy a good munch! My gastronomic delight was, however, suddenly interrupted by a voice from the doorway, "Elsie Giles, what are you doing?" Not one whit abashed, I replied, innocently, "Can't find the lentils anywhere, Miss Slade". Dear Miss Slade! Apart from an imposed ban on entering the cupboard, she allowed me to go unpunished. Discipline was not, perhaps, her strongest point, but she was a kindly soul. After a year or so she left to get married and was replaced by Miss Williams, who was made of much sterner stuff. She stood for no nonsense and under her efficient regime even my dubious standards of cookery improved, though I dropped the subject altogether in the end "to concentrate on Latin"! That, at any rate, was my excuse.

We had nine different biology teachers during my time. Most of their tenures were short-lived and dreadful. One I remember had a terrible lisp; to hear her pronounce the word "rhizome" was mental agony. Another was so boring that virtually no-one listened to her and I can only with some difficulty remember her name, which for obvious reasons I will not quote. Mrs. Roberts was much better; she was pretty, vivacious and wore very fashionable clothes. I liked her, although I fear her opinion of me was equivocal: I well remember her lecturing me for alleged inattention in class and telling me I should fail my end-of-term exams. Stung into activity, I responded by achieving a mark of 88%, which to my delight appeared to annoy her very much.

In our fifth year we acquired a male biology teacher. Mr. Stevens was very young; he was good-looking with very blue eyes and we girls nearly all imagined ourselves in love with him. He must at times have found our adulation extremely irritating, expressed as it was mainly by fits of giggling in class and other attention-seeking forms of teenage behaviour.

My favourite teacher in my first year, however, was a certain Miss Alder - a small, wiry lady who usually dressed in a tartan kilt, and who kept her hair very unsuccessfully in a large untidy roll, from which long wisps would escape and fall down over her shoulders. Miss Alder, on whom I developed quite a crush for a term or so, had a gentle, quiet manner: more important, she taught almost exclusively the subjects I liked best, including drama. Under her direction we put on three end-of-term plays during our first year. In one of them (with an all-girl cast) I was given the role of Peter Quince in an abbreviated version of "Midsummer Night's Dream". Along with the other rude mechanicals I was required to wear an inverted Hessian sack, with holes cut out for the neck and arms. These chafed our skins terribly and we itched for days afterwards, but the play was voted a great success.

I loved drama, both in class and in performance, and usually contrived to win myself a speaking role in the operettas which the Junior School performed annually for parents, just before Christmas time. I particularly remember one of these productions: a piece called "Jan of Windmill Land". It was, in retrospect, a somewhat mawkish bit of theatre, though it contained some rather pretty songs and dances, and lent itself to attractive costumes, the male part of the chorus being decked out in patched baggy trousers and clogs, the girls in traditional

Dutch costumes with starched white bonnets. I was cast, however, not as a pretty little Dutch girl but, clad in drooping black muslin, as a wicked fairy. My partner in crime was a slightly younger girl named Paddy Rogers: thus it came about that I was invited to Paddy's house to tea one Monday, in order that we might rehearse our scenes together. The occasion must have been a success, for it was repeated every Monday for almost the whole of the autumn term.

The Rogers family, from my standpoint at any rate, were extremely well-off. Paddy's father was a bookmaker, and a member of the Borough Council. Her mother, an inexhaustible charity worker, was chairman of innumerable committees in the town. They lived in considerable comfort "above the shop". I was intrigued by their life-style, which seemed to me quite sumptuous. They had, for instance, a "lounge" rather than a plain sitting room. Furthermore, the said lounge was carpeted, instead of having shabby lino and old rugs on the floor. I have cause to remember that room very well indeed, for it was there we rehearsed, Monday after Monday that autumn, until a more competently evil pair of fairies could not have been found anywhere!

On the night of the first performance we were given make-up to match our characters. Paddy's mother declared to mine that she had "almost fainted" with horror when we came on stage. Nevertheless, we were a hit with the audience and got a great deal of applause for our pantomime-style over-acting.

Possibly by way of compensation for her daughter having to look less than glamorous in the play, Paddy's mother made her, the following spring, a new dress for Flora Day. We had by then arrived in the era of Dior's "New Look" and that dress was more "New Look" than anything we had yet come across. It was, of course, white - I think it was made of nylon - with yards of material in the skirt: none of us had ever seen anything so lavish. With red poppies in her waist-length hair, Paddy stole the show again, much to the annoyance of some of the senior girls, who thought she was getting above herself, an opinion regrettably reinforced when it was learned that the Rogers were going abroad for their summer holiday-something no-one local had done since before the War, and few had done then.

My own summer holidays followed the same safe and regular pattern they always had done. Most days were spent on the beach, and I suppose we never really appreciated the fact that the beach was there in easy walking distance of home. Often we took our lunch and tea with us - usually arriving home famished at about three thirty in the afternoon! Sometimes we swam in the harbour, which was more filthy than we realised, but I do not remember that anyone was any the worse of it. In the evenings, when the tide was high, the boys used to jump off the quays to show off their swimming skills, whilst we paraded about pretending not to notice them, hoping the while that they would notice us. They rarely did. Elizabeth Sampson sometimes swam with the boys, which we thought very daring of her, though not so daring as the fact that she wore a two-piece bathing costume, something of which most of our mothers strongly disapproved.

On dull, damp or chilly days, when the weather was unsuitable for the beach, we would go for walks - often to Loe Bar, a favourite haunt of mine. I was very keen on the Arthurian legends at that time, and was convinced (mainly by Tennyson's poem) that Loe Pool was the place where Excalibur had been cast into the water. If I was alone on the bar, I would half expect to see an arm "clothed in white samite" rising from the Pool, brandishing a sword with a jewelled hilt. Sadly, this never transpired, but part of the romance of early youth was the supposition that it might. I even wrote a poem "The Return of Arthur" proclaiming my expectations of this happening. In the meantime I learned the names of some of the rarer plants which grow on Loe Bar, and familiarised myself with badger tracks around the Pool's edge.

We did have a few outings during the course of the summer - the same ones, every year. One of my favourites was an excursion to Tangies (described in detail in "Seagull Morning") and I would wander its meadows with my friend Joyce who lived there, often picking blackberries in jam jars. It was on one such walk that she told me about her boyfriend, Jack, whom she subsequently married. Jack, a local young farmer, belonged as Joyce did to the lovely little Methodist Chapel at Degibna. Their subsequent married life, sadly cut short by Jack's untimely illness and early death, seemed to me idyllic, living as they did in a farmhouse on the very shores of Loe Pool: their working days governed by the demands of the farm and the changing of the seasons: their leisure hours focussed on the life of the chapel they both loved so much.

But this was all still in the future during our late summer wanderings in the mid 1940s. Looking back, they were dream days. If the weather turned poor, Joyce would play the piano in the sitting room and we would sing songs from the News Chronicle Song Book, or hymns from the Methodist Hymn Book. We saw nothing odd in this somewhat Victorian pastime. I longed to be able to play the piano myself, but alas! there was no room for a piano in our damp little sitting room at home, nor any spare cash to pay for lessons. It is still my intention to learn to play the piano one day!

Thus passed the summer - every year we visited Uncle Norman at Medlyn Moor, and Uncle Henry at Devoran, as we had done throughout my childhood. We might go to Falmouth or, more likely, to Penzance. I preferred Falmouth because of Marks and Spencers; besides, Penzance always smelled strongly of gasworks and made one feel slightly sick. Our visits there were usually for the purpose of buying sensible shoes for the autumn term, or a new gym-slip, or some other dreary necessity such as socks or underwear. The latter was particularly dull and, with hindsight, embarrassing. You were expected to wear a vest - some of the girls with whom I shared the school changing rooms actually had vests with sleeves! We also wore a garment known as a liberty bodice - though there was nothing in the least liberating about this constricting piece of clothing, the exact purpose of which I never fully understood: it was probably meant to be a junior precursor of the corset! My mother told me that when she was a girl liberty bodices had suspenders attached to them, and held up the thick black stockings they wore to school. We were at least spared that discomfort. At the age of twelve I had begun to need to wear a bra, but it was frowned upon to have such an adult piece of equipment at such an early age, and I had to endure the hated liberty bodice for a further twelve months until my mother decided that at thirteen necessity must prevail and my underpinnings were adjusted accordingly. The vest was not so easily discarded, though most of us refused to wear them in the summer months.

The autumn term at school brought with it Speech Day and Prizegiving, normally held in November in those days. Visually this was a spectacular affair; the school hall polished to perfection and decorated with extravagant displays of the incurved chrysanthemums which were coming into high fashion at that time; pink and yellow and bronze, and smelling of autumn; crisp and clean and slightly bitter. Against this floral backdrop the staff, decked out in their academic hoods and mortar boards as well as the gowns they always wore in class, paraded in with the visiting celebrities who were due to make speeches and present prizes. I am sorry to recall that most of these worthies had little or no talent for public speaking, particularly to an audience of children and young people. One notable exception to this was His Honour Judge Scobell Armstrong, who presented the prizes at my very first Speech Day. His talk, aimed at some of the older pupils (we were always "pupils" not "students" in those days, and quite rightly so) nonetheless came across with some force to those of us who were younger. "Bad language" I remember him saying "springs principally from lack of vocabulary". I had never viewed the matter that way before but resolved, quietly, that I should never lack vocabulary. This was no hardship, for words fascinated me, then as now. In another location, at a later date, I heard Judge Scobell Armstrong take part in a debate about the use of alcohol, and on that occasion he declared "fond as I am of a glass of claret, if I thought that my example would cause anyone to become a drunk, then I would abandon the practice forthwith".

This uncompromising attitude to social mores and problems still dominated adult thinking at that time, at least in the circles in which we were growing up. The "shades of grey" with which one comes into contact later in life - and nowadays probably much earlier than we did - seemed non-existent. There was black and there was white; right and wrong. School staff, parents, Sunday School teachers, preachers - all combined forces to make sure we knew which was which, even if we did not always readily embrace the correct one.

There was, however, always the same sharp line between what were perceived as the more serious forms of wrongdoing - drinking, for instance, or "going all the way" with the opposite sex - and the more acceptable forms of youthful villainy, such as acting the fool in class, at which latter activity I regret to record I had become adept. Looking back, one wonders why one engaged in such silly behaviour, and what deep-seated psychological disorders motivated it, but it all seemed perfectly natural at the time. It was the way to be - it gained you status amongst your peer group, especially those who were too timid to behave badly themselves, but derived vicarious delight from the exploits of those of us who were prepared to risk the wrath of authority to create what passed for amusing scenes in the classroom. Thus, far from being deflated by public reprimand for some misdemeanour, I would actually experience a sense of triumph. Being sent to the headmistress was a high point: it marked me out as a dare-devil, and outstandingly wicked! There were, I regret to record, a number of such occasions. Perhaps the most ridiculous of them all - and maybe it was a turning point in my attitude to the thing - was when I had grown very tall for my age and a new headmistress, diminutive of stature, had taken office. She required me to recount my misdeeds - a requirement with which I was only too happy to comply. Then, gazing up at my five foot six from her four foot eleven, she reproached me with, "That was naughty of you, wasn't it?". Lost for a suitable reply, I affected contrition, the while storing the details of the incident ready to indulge my talent for mimicry amongst my cronies in the cloakroom. "That was naughty of you, wasn't it?" became a catch-phrase for the whole of the rest of that term.

Helston Grammar was a *little* school, even by the standards of the age. There were only a couple of hundred pupils at any one time, and everyone tended to know everyone else, which was a good thing. In those days, however, most children still stayed in their village schools until they reached the age of fourteen, and then went to work in local shops, or the net loft, or the fish factory (where they processed pilchards, still being caught in droves and landed in Porthleven harbour). Boys went fishing, or farming, or became apprenticed to carpenters, masons and shipbuilders. Some became electricians - a growth industry, though I had classmates from the country villages who still lived in homes lit by Tilley lamps, their mothers cooking exclusively on Cornish ranges, known as "slabs". At eighteen, the boys went off to do their National Service for two years. Some learned their trade during that time - others, less lucky, passed a wasteful period of their lives performing contrived and unnecessary chores. At twenty they would return home, perhaps a little broader-minded than they had been when they went away. At that point of time they would start going out regularly with a particular girl, marry at twenty-two or three, and settle down to domestic bliss, or otherwise, as the case might be. Life was not uncomfortable, and was improving all the time, the further we got from the end of the war. Aspirations, however, were not noticeably high, and things tended to go on much as they always had done.

There were, nevertheless, some significant changes. Our "year" for instance, was the first Grammar School intake under the terms of the 1944 Education Act, when fee-paying in many of the state Grammar Schools was abolished, and everyone had to pass the scholarship exam to gain entry. This initially posed some problems for the school staff: thitherto they had simply put the "scholarship" people into one form and the fee-payers who had passed a rather less demanding "entrance exam", into another. Now they had to find a new way of sorting out the sheep and the goats. They did it, that year at least, by making us all sit another exam on our first day. This somewhat un-nerving experience was rendered the more so by virtue of it taking place in the chemistry lab - a strange, totally new environment for us, smelling of rotten eggs and full of huge glass bottles labelled "Hydrochloric Acid" and suchlike, with Bunsen burners in front of us on the benches, giving off the inevitable faint reek of gas.

That chemistry lab became our home for the first school year. Form rooms were in short supply and were allocated mainly to senior classes. We therefore found ourselves with no desks in which to store our books, but instead had to stack them on shelves in a large open cupboard in the corridor. This could cause considerable mayhem as the people whose books were on the top shelf tried to climb up to reach them, while those fortunate enough to be allocated spaces lower down were attempting to extract from their own bundles the necessities of the day. Fights not infrequently broke out, sometimes resulting in lines, or an hour's detention after school. The latter was quite a problem in times when most homes had no telephone: you had to try to let your mother know that you would be an hour late home - further, of course, you had to face her wrath when you got there.

For the most part, I was extremely happy at Helston Grammar, and I think most of my contemporaries were also. Remembering those days is rather like looking into a kaleidoscope of ever-changing patterns; sights and sounds and smells which, because you were young and they were new to you, are never forgotten. Deep in the bins of memory, they endure: the clouds of chalk dust as the blackboards were cleaned ready for the next lesson: the vase of narcissi outside the door of the room where Shimmy was teaching (he could not bear the smell of narcissi) the fragrance of the polish on the first day of term; the slightly acrid scent of flowering currant near the girls' entrance door in the spring; the unappetising odours from the school kitchen.

One should not, perhaps, denigrate the kitchen staff too severely. They were wrestling with post-war shortages, including, one term, a total dearth of potatoes, when macaroni was served as the principal accompaniment to every meal - macaroni devoid of any sort of sauce, moreover. This was, I suppose, unavoidable - however, there is a persistent memory of greasy gravy, lumpy custard, bits of meat which seemed to consist largely of gristle, soggy cabbage and helpings of "steamed stodge" - wet and unpalatable - reminiscent of papier maché in the making.

The head cook was Mrs. Flynn - a stout, bustling lady with a sharp tongue and fingers stained with nicotine - for, like her husband, who was the school caretaker, she was a fairly heavy smoker. Mr. Flynn fascinated me: years later I even wrote a poem about him. He would wander around the school - a Woodbine between his lips as like as not, and an enormous broom in his hands. These tools of his trade were accessorised by a large tin of a substance called "Dusmo", which he sprinkled on the floors before sweeping them at a leisurely pace. Flynn always appeared to me to be half asleep. His wife, however, was a much more dynamic and bustling character, very much in control in the kitchen. She had a less-than-endearing habit of licking her fingers if they became sticky whilst serving lunches, and then using those same fingers to pick up something to put on the next person's plate.

In spite of all this, however, there were boys who queued up for extras with monotonous regularity; some of them came from what would nowadays be called "deprived backgrounds". They too were something of a novelty in the school; before 1945 the annual intake had consisted mainly of the children of reasonably moneyed people, who could without too much difficulty cope with the strain of affording the uniform. My own parents had a considerable struggle over this expense, but my mother refused to allow me to apply for the small amount of available help - this because there was great snobbery in the school and if it became known that you "had the allowance" you tended to be despised and ostracised by some of the better-off. So my mother cleaned houses and served in shops, and rubbed her fingers raw making broccoli nets to earn the money to buy the regulation items, which were many. Perhaps because I knew they were so hard-bought I tended to be sentimental about them. I still have in my possession some bits of school uniform - a tie, a blazer badge - a beret - and my very first school hat, an item of indescribable design, resembling most closely a pudding basin, but without being really recognisable as any shape at all.

The great argument in favour of a school uniform is that it is a good leveller. Your parents can be immensely wealthy or extremely poor - the circumstance is not readily discernible when you are clad in a shapeless navy-blue tunic exactly like those being worn by all your contemporaries.

By the time we reached our second year, of course, we had begun to loathe our uniforms, the novelty of which had decidedly worn off. We especially detested the knickers - navy blue, designed with long legs, which drooped in a most unattractive and unprovocative manner halfway down to our knees! We learned to hoist them up to the tops of our thighs to get them out of the way. The end result of this exercise was that the folds of material flapped around our backsides when we pranced about in the gym wearing them.

It was a punishable offence to wear knickers of any other colour or style, though in the summer most of us disobeyed this stricture whenever we thought we could get away with it. I remember this to my cost because of one of the most embarrassing incidents in my young life.

24

It was Sports Day. I had reached the finals of the Junior High Jump, and expected to perform on the school field before an admiring audience of parents, clad in a fetching pair of regulation green shorts. I decided not to wear the hated navy blues underneath, and donned instead in what was, at the time, a popular shade of pale pink. Alas! During the night it had rained heavily and word was brought round the form rooms to the effect that the field was slippery and would be unsafe for the High Jump. Those taking part were summoned to the gym during the morning. Shorts - the correct attire for the field - would not be worn. Navy knickers - regulation for the gym - would. I had none available, and to my shame and horror had to take part in the High Jump final wearing pink knickers! With boys watching! Somewhat to my relief, I was given no punishment for this sartorial offence - I think the senior mistress realised that the incident itself was punishment enough. My performance, furthermore, was affected by my embarrassment. I jumped well below my best and finished third. I have never since felt quite the same about pink knickers!

During my third year at Helston Grammar there occurred one of those life-changing events which you do not recognise as such until years afterwards. Miss Rowe, who taught English, left to take up a post in a Methodist Girls' Boarding School somewhere up-country - a position to which she was eminently suited and where I am sure she did well. She was succeeded by one Ken Nicholson, a rangy, loose-limbed Scotsman with a face rather like that of an eagle and a thatch of untidy hair which tended to flop forward over his eyes. He dressed somewhat badly in an elderly brown suit which looked suspiciously like a demob issue - while his academic gown was never quite properly on his shoulders, and in consequence flapped wildly about him as he strode along the school corridors with his curious loping gait. This man was to exert such an influence on my life (and probably upon the lives of many others) that I should never be quite the same again after knowing him. He was, first and foremost, a fine teacher. He had that knack of letting you chat about any subject, and you would think you had side-tracked him; then at the end of the lesson you would realise that he had got his point across without your having noticed. He was an accomplished actor; a poet, a considerable classical scholar and what is generally known as "a character". He would stride into the room looking fierce and announce "I'm in a foul temper - don't get me out of it, I want to save some for 4B" - or some such similar statement. His lessons were filled with laughter - argument - even uproar on occasions - but his class was never beyond his control and he had the one great pre-requisite of the successful teacher - the ability to inspire! Conventional he was not; boring he never was; there were those members of staff, we sensed, who did not love him as we did - but his brilliance rubbed off on those around him so that even the dimmest star in our particular firmament would shine somewhat brighter under his ministrations.

Ken Nicholson discovered that I wrote poetry. He encouraged this: I still have a small volume of my early poems that he took the trouble to have typed for me, and of which he kept a copy for himself. I hope they brought him some joy: it was a thrill to me that he thought them worthy of keeping. When I become discouraged with my literary efforts, even now, I can sometimes feel his benign spirit standing behind my shoulder encouraging me to keep trying to produce something worth-while.

For me, therefore, there was school and there was Nicholson, who contrived to transcend his pedantic calling in a truly remarkable fashion, and by some inner magic to imbue even Latin grammar with glory and to turn any ordinary English lesson into the highlight of a day. I owe him an eternal debt of gratitude, for he fostered in me a love affair with words which was to remain with me throughout my life.

Nicholson invited the entire cast of the school play to his house one Christmas: socially gauche and uneasy, I spent the entire evening playing with his dog on the sitting room floor whilst my fellow-Thespians made polite conversation and attempted sophisticated behaviour. In an attempt to compensate for my lack of social skills, I wrote a fulsome letter of thanks the next day. I hope the Nicholsons understood: indeed, I am sure they did, for they were a warm-hearted and kindly couple. Sadly, they left Cornwall after only a few years to seek treatment in London for the arthritis which was slowly crippling her, and to which the Cornish winters were making their own inexorable contribution. I was glad that by then I was no longer at school - it would have been unbearable to me without the influence of Nicholson to leaven the lump of learning.

The fact of my leaving at sixteen was, however, a source of genuine heartache, both to me and to some of those who had the dubious privilege of teaching me, none of whom appeared to desire my premature departure. A nuisance I undoubtedly was; bright; cheeky; lazy; my homework scamped on summer evenings so that I could go down and wander about the quays and the pier, chatting with friends and eyeing the opposite sex (without any noticeable effect)! I nevertheless had a good brain and would no doubt have benefited greatly from the disciplines of a spell in the Sixth Form, followed by University. The reasons this did not happen were complex and largely, if not entirely, beyond my control. There is no more to be said about it, except perhaps that problems which look like mountains when one is sixteen appear as molehills forty or fifty years later. But who is wise at sixteen? And there have been many as foolish as I was. Life, however, still had a great deal to offer me as I reluctantly walked for the last time down the cinder path and took the four-twenty bus home that July afternoon of 1950.

There is one incident relating to that time which stands out in my memory. It was customary for school leavers to assemble outside the headmaster's office on the day of their departures. Each was then seen individually by the head himself and wished well. Coming out from my turn I met a boy called George Angell going in. He was to take up an engineering apprenticeship in Falmouth Docks, and I was to do a Commercial Course at Falmouth "Tech". "We'll be seeing each other then" I said. "Yes" he replied. "I'll look out for you in Falmouth". Two days later he was dead, struck on the head by a cricket ball whilst playing for his village side, Porkellis. His death caused a minor sensation in the national press, and I learned of it from my father's copy of the "Daily Herald". It was a most sobering experience; a strangely tragic ending to a story which - like most old-fashioned school stories - was largely comedy from beginning to end and which is still remembered with something akin to delight.

Flynn

Do you remember Flynn?
With his drooping Woodbine
And his tin
Of Dusmo
That big, soft broom
That he carried
Like a staff of office
From room to room,
And the big, soft shoes,
Grey,
Like floormops
And the way
His hair sprouted
Like the tufts of a scrubbing brush
And the check-duster shirt,
Worn
Like a badge of rank?
You could have sworn
That he was born
To be a school caretaker.
Flynn never hurried –
Was never happy –

Nor ever sad, either.
He never spoke to you
But growled
Between his teeth,
Stained brown with nicotine
As all his fingers were.
Flynn was never heard to laugh,
Never seen to smile.
A most unmemorable man –
And easy to forget.
I suppose he died
Long ago
It is a quarter of a century
Since last I saw him
Yet
A night or two ago
I unaccountably
Dreamed about Flynn

Elsie Balme
c. 1975

CHAPTER 2

"Climbing the Steps"

IT is fashionable nowadays for school-leavers to take a "Gap Year", during which they may do a variety of worthy or interesting things - or nothing at all. Whilst no such indulgence existed officially in my time, my three-term sojourn at Falmouth Technical Institute was, in a sense, my "Gap Year", bringing with it at one and the same time both many new and worth-while experiences, and a previously undreamed-of degree of idleness.

The object of the exercise was to acquire some sort of work qualification - basic secretarial skills, book-keeping, shorthand and typing. Three of us from Helston Grammar had opted for the course, of whom I was one. At the time I had no intention whatsoever of becoming a "mere secretary", having aspirations to a high-flying career in journalism, to which I was totally unsuited, and which like most of my young dreams was destined to come to nothing, though ironically enough, the despised shorthand and typing were to stand me in good stead all through life. The former came easily to me: the latter decidedly less so. Still tending to lack manual dexterity, it took me a long time to teach my errant fingers to move around the keyboard with any degree of accuracy, and I spent many frustrating hours pounding out the basic exercises. I took comfort in the fact that I was by no means alone in this difficulty, part of which was engendered by the collection of ancient, heavy and unwieldy machines with which the Tech typing room was equipped. There were several Remingtons of pre-war vintage, and an old Underwood which must have dated from the nineteen twenties. One fairly decent Olympia was always pounced upon by whoever managed to get through the door first; the rest of us squabbled over half a dozen khaki-coloured Bar-Locks (ex War Department issue) of dubious quality but having at least the merit of being slightly less cumbersome than the Remingtons under our inexperienced and aching fingers.

Learning to type on these machines had a curious physical effect: to this day I have incurving little fingers on both hands, the distortion caused by slamming them down hard on the "A", the semi-colon, the "P" the "Q" the "Z" and the full-stop. The same bent-finger phenomenon is shared by many of my generation who attended commercial schools in the early post-war era, before ergonomically designed keys eased some of the pressure on sore fingertips; before electric typewriters had properly come on to the market, and the word "computer" had hardly made it to the most advanced dictionary.

Our instructor for both shorthand and typing was a Mrs. Thomas - a voluble Welsh lady, short of stature and vast of girth, so that she seemed as round as she was tall. Her hair was dyed a peculiarly bright blonde and her manner was dramatic, involving huge gestures. Her diction, however, was exquisite and her speaking voice would have marked her out as a female counterpart of Richard Burton, had the latter been famous at that time. Mrs. T. was loquacious and excitable: her personality was so pronounced that anyone with even a modicum of talent for mimicry found her an easy subject. Thus there came the day when she peered into a room where some second-year students were supposedly working unsupervised. "Bernice, what are you doing?" she demanded in ringing tones. "Dictating, Mrs. Thomas", replied the unabashed Bernice. There was a short pause, followed by, "Do I wave my arms about like that when I dictate?" To which there was no reply that could be both honest and tactful, for Mrs. Thomas' arms indeed waved like the sails of a windmill on most occasions.

She billowed out of our lives at the end of our first term, to be replaced by Mrs. Barnett. It was rather like chalk replacing cheese. Mrs. B. was extremely tall and very thin. She was quiet and reserved of manner, softly spoken, not in the least given to any sort of extravagant gesture, but with a kind of restrained refinement about her which was largely wasted on most of her students. She was a journalist turned author, and I knew her quite well because, like me, she lived in Porthleven, where her novel "Wind from the South" had sold reasonably well, but caused a minor furore because of its rather obvious parallels to a local fishing disaster.

Mrs. B. was not in the best of health at the time and resigned after a very short tenure of office, to be succeeded by Mrs. Wilde - brisk, efficient, tough and very much in charge of things, forcing us to keep up the pace - literally so in shorthand, in which by the end of the year we were supposed to attain a minimum speed of one hundred words a minute. I managed to achieve this without a great deal of difficulty: not everyone did, however. In the meantime, we struggled on with the typewriters, accompanied by excruciating music from an ancient gramophone. The specially-designed records were supposed to help us become more rhythmic in our use of the keyboard, and were punctuated at regular intervals by a sepulchral female voice announcing "Carriage....Return". All this caused considerable annoyance to whichever group of male day-release students was trying to work in the room next door: the walls were in fact not walls at all but screens, and were totally unsoundproof.

The whole of the building in which we were housed had come as what nowadays would be termed a culture shock after Helston Grammar. The latter, a relatively new building, which had only opened in 1939, was in its time a model of how a well-designed school should look. The floors were parquet and glowed with polish: the form-rooms airy and well-lit; there was a fine gymnasium, a library which was little short of luxurious; a purpose-built art room, a geography room, and of course chemistry and physics labs, domestic science room and woodwork room, all properly equipped with whatever had been deemed necessary at the time of the school's opening, and whatever more had been able to be added in spite of the interference of the war. If the classrooms were a little on the chilly side in winter, this was probably due more to fuel shortages than to any defect in the actual heating system.

By contrast, Falmouth Tech was temporarily housed in two shabby old buildings the best part of a mile apart from each other, the main one being in Killigrew Street. From the outside, that building was little short of ostentatious, having a huge front portico with fat Greek-style columns spaced out along it. Inside, however, it had manifestly not been designed for the purpose for which it had come to be used, and it tended to be cramped, though less so than its satellite, a former primary school set on Smithick Hill, slap in the middle of what in those days was one of the toughest areas in that generally rugged seaport of Falmouth. The Smithick building housed the commercial department, cheek-by-jowl with such activities as engineering and brick-laying. It boasted few facilities - even the toilets were out of doors, round the corner at the far end of the yard. This could cause considerable embarrassment if you had to cross that yard when a brick-laying class was going on - not only were you likely to get wolf whistles and catcalls, but on particularly rowdy days you might find a lump of wet cement landing - if you were lucky - at your feet or - if you were not - on your shoulder or in the small of your back. Neither was there anywhere, other than the staff room, to wash your hands. It was decidedly not what we were used to, and we deplored it. Indoors, there were no proper desks: we sat squashed-in three to a trestle table, our work and equipment spilling over into each other's spaces. Heating was all but non-existent; the floors were utilitarian wooden planks which had presumably been kept scrubbed in their youth - but that had been long ago.

There was a sense, therefore, in which our brief sojourn at Tech was an exercise in self-preservation and survival. We became, moreover, very fit, though I have to say I sorely missed the gym! However, our bus would arrive on Falmouth Moor at three minutes to nine in the morning - classes began at nine. The quickest way to cover the distance was up that enormous flight of steps known as Jacob's Ladder - after some puffing and blowing in the early weeks, we learned to run from the bottom to the top and still not be out of breath when we arrived in Smithick.

The bus journey itself was a tedious enough affair, taking an hour and a half each morning from Porthleven Square to Falmouth, stopping at every hamlet and most farm gates en route. I was never a very committed knitter, but I knitted at least three sweaters on those bus journeys to alleviate the monotony.

Knitting, if you were wise, was put safely away before you reached Penryn, where the bus was boarded by an assortment of high-spirited young men - some bound, like ourselves, for the Tech, others for Falmouth Grammar. Amongst the latter was one Roger Hosen, destined for fame in the world of Rugby, but at that time chiefly notable for a school cap which seemed glued to the back of his head, where it perched almost vertically, yet never fell off.

Penryn held a peculiar fascination for me. To begin with, every other building seemed to be a public house - so much so that I seriously wondered why they had not run out of appropriate names for so many hostelries. I gathered that there was, at the time, a great deal of drunkenness in the town, especially on Saturday nights. To counter this, however, there appeared to be a huge community spirit, something which seemed to be much less obvious in Falmouth - presumably because of its larger size and more disparate population. Penryn people supported their own town vociferously - their war-cry of "Up the Borough" was heard on numerous occasions, many of them, though not all, to do with sport.

There were and indeed are a number of fine buildings in "the Borough". In those days most of them looked fairly seedy, not having been restored for many years and probably never even painted during the war. Regeneration of the town in recent times has effected quite a transformation, and parts of Penryn are architecturally impressive. I cannot say, however, that the main street in the autumn of 1950 gave quite such a pleasing impression. The houses there were grim, dingy and closely crammed together, as though huddled for warmth against the fog which seemed to blow up from the river continually. I used to say, somewhat unkindly, that the acid test of whether you really loved a man would be whether you were prepared to live with him in the main street of Penryn.

I was told on one occasion about the horse-drawn fire-engine which was once the pride of The Borough. Unfortunately, the horse employed to pull it was a difficult catch, and apparently more than one fire took firm hold whilst breathless firemen pursued the intractable animal round and round its field, trying in vain to put a halter on it.

Sometimes, on summer afternoons, we would walk round the back roads to Penryn after classes, and catch the bus home from there. This reduced the time spent in the stuffy confines of public transport, though the homeward journey was rather quicker than the morning one, taking just over an hour in all. This was sufficient to enable most of one's homework to be done before arriving home, leaving the whole evening free for personal pursuits. It was all delightfully undemanding, and life required very little mental effort at that stage.

This quickly became apparent, especially to our English tutor, Mr. Brown, who decided that I would be better occupied editing the Tech Magazine than re-working exercises in English Grammar with which I was already more than familiar. This decision led to one of the most delightful episodes of that year, as the "Tech Review" (Vol.1 Edition 1) took shape. With hindsight, it has to be admitted that this crude publication was neither erudite nor particularly entertaining, except perhaps to those contributors who saw their work in print for the first (and probably the last) time. The subject matter was, for the most part, unutterably boring and if the spelling and grammar seemed reasonably competent, it was because every article included had been rigorously edited - spellings corrected and the worst grammatical excesses ironed out. Thus I spent many enjoyable hours playing at being an editor, and found it extremely fulfilling, even if it did little to expand my own small fund of knowledge. My co-editors and I (we had formed a committee to produce the magazine) were nevertheless proud of the result. One article, at least, had the merit of being amusing, though perhaps not to those whose work was included in it. Entitled "Smithigrews" (from a fusion of the addresses "Smithick" and "Killigrew") it was a fine collection of howlers from (un-named) people's essays - and there were plenty from which to choose. "Aluminium is a useful metal because it expands when it is contracting" was one prime example. Another, from an essay on "Wind in the Willows" read "Toad, when he saw the first motor car, immediately went into a comma (sic) and didn't come out until he had had one". No-one was ever completely sure what the unfortunate writer had in mind on this occasion, but it gave rise to considerable amusement.

Perhaps it was as well that in that hazily-remembered year of idleness and new experience, we were easily amused. Money was tight, and we could not afford to pay for our entertainment. Indeed, I can remember only one occasion during the entire three terms when I afforded to stay behind after classes to go to the cinema in Falmouth. The film, if I remember correctly, was showing at the Odeon and was "Sunset Boulevard" starring Gloria Swanson. I found it disappointing, and hardly worth the one-and-nine for the seat, or the scramble to catch the last bus home. I would not have admitted it at the time, but I was terrified of missing that bus and having to take an unaffordable taxi all the way to Helston. This was one of my reasons for opting out of the "extra studies" evening classes held at the Tech for our benefit each Monday; another was my suspicion that there was in fact little extra to be learned on these occasions. In the sublime arrogance of someone in her mid-teens with a fairly impressive list of exam successes already notched up I had, I believed, more interesting things to do with my time.

Falmouth itself, however, seemed an extremely exciting place to me, comparing very favourably with Penzance and even more so with Helston, which in those days was still a rather sleepy, if not unpleasant, little market town, and did not boast so much as a branch of Woolworths to enliven the shopping scene. Falmouth, by contrast, seemed full of exciting shops and glamorous goods. Even though we could not often afford to buy anything, we could while away our lunch hours window-shopping along Market Street, Church Street and Arwenack Street. Needless to say, our favourite haunts were those emporia which sold clothes. There was, for example, a recently-opened branch of Richard Shops, which we should have described as "trendy" had the word been in parlance at the time. It was there that I spent my Christmas money on an ultra-fashionable new skirt with a long and rather seductive slit up the back, only to be ordered by my mother to return it to the shop and exchange it for "something more suitable". I did as required, not without some underlying resentment, and suffered such intense embarrassment that I avoided Richard Shops for weeks. Other favourite lunchtime viewing was provided by stores such as Wilsons, (a close rival to Richard Shops) Cox and Horder (expensive but stylish) and of course, Marks and Spencer, where you could take refuge from the rain and browse to your hearts' content among the rails of skirts, frocks, and exquisite lingerie! To us, newly-liberated from our hated navy-blue gymslips, merely looking at these things was a joy and a delight.

It must have been around this same time that I developed what was to be a lifelong fascination with jewellers' windows, the sparkle and glitter of which still have the power to draw me like a magnet as I walk through a town centre. I made daily inspections of my personal favourites: in particular I adored the Cornish

Stone Shop in Market Street, deriving immense pleasure from the brilliantly lit stones on their beds of black velvet.

Bookshops, also, were passable entertainment, though in those early post-war years they tended not to be particularly well-stocked and the covers of the books were for the most part still rather utilitarian and austere. There were a couple of second-hand bookshops, but I was never able to bring myself to care greatly for second-hand books, disliking the smell of them, amongst other things. Neither was I much drawn in those days to places like Maggs famous print shop, though I always loved the bow-windows and the quaint air they lent to that part of the street.

On fine days we would forsake the town centre and explore the waterfront, or wander through the innumerable "opes" and alleys behind the main street, or walk out Woodlane and down to Gyllyngvase beach, where once a week in the summer we were set free to swim on Wednesday afternoons, in compliance with the rules about the provision of physical exercise, always difficult to provide in the cramped buildings where our further education was taking place.

These excursions round the town in the lunch hour took place, however, as much from necessity as from choice. Neither the Killigrew nor the Smithick premises boasted a canteen; the latter was, in any event, locked up from 12 noon to 1 pm, and we were not permitted to remain inside. We became adept at locating cheap lunches -bags of chips from the Gem Cafe in Quarry Hill, for instance, or sandwiches or salad rolls (threepence each in the currency of the time) from Woolworths' Snack Bar, where we listened with a mixture of prim horror and prurient fascination to the waitresses recounting to each other their previous nights' amorous exploits with deck-hands off visiting ships. Looking back, I realise that most of these girls were little more than my own age - one or two of them possibly rather younger than I. It was a mark of my erstwhile naiveté that I regarded them as "older". Certainly they seemed to inhabit another world from my own safe, slightly stuffy and over-protected environment. These "Woolworths' girls" as we collectively referred to them, were by comparison liberated, daring and, viewed in retrospect, perhaps rather more genuinely alive than we were, though speaking for myself I did not at the time envy their racy lifestyles. However, it remains a gap in my education that I never did go out with a deck-hand from any vessel moored in Falmouth Docks!

Life generally was enlivened by the presence of the docks, and the perpetual activity of them: the whole town seemed to vibrate with animation from that source, and there were always ships coming and going for re-fits. From the wall outside the back of Smithick School you could look down over that whole great spread of maritime industry and across the harbour towards Flushing: there was always something interesting and exciting going on.

Like most seaboard towns, Falmouth had its fair share of local characters. One whom I well remember was "Cowboy" Mitchell, who lived somewhere in the vicinity of Smithick, and whom we consequently saw quite often. Cowboy was a quiet enough man most of the time, but he had a disconcerting habit of suddenly bursting from a walk into an exaggerated gallop, firing an imaginary gun at startled passers-by and yelling obscenities. This behaviour would have been odd enough in a badly brought up boy, but Cowboy must have been well over sixty years old when we knew him. We were given to understand that he suffered from some kind of mental disturbance, and, needless to say, spent a great deal of time in the cinema, watching Westerns. Some of the Tech boys teased him unmercifully, which was cruel; unfortunately they loved to "get him going" as they crudely put it, and would goad him into a rage to see what he might do next. His great saving grace was his fondness for cats, of which he kept a number, and in whose company he seemed happier and more contented than he did amongst his fellow human beings. No doubt there is a lesson to be learned from this. Certainly for most people, of whom I am one, cats are a soothing influence in a pressured existence.

Another individual I well remember from those days was one Ronnie Webb, who did not live in the town, but seemed to haunt it. He kept a smallholding in Sevorgan, where he tended a number of goats. He would come into Falmouth on the bus and park himself at the snack bar in Woolworths, chatting up the girls there, who were not inclined to be over-impressed by this middle-aged Lothario in thick glasses, beret and farm clothing which always smelled of billy-goat - admittedly an occupational hazard for anyone working with these rather pungent creatures. It is a well-recorded fact, however, that entering Woolworths one wet winter lunchtime, my friend Sylvia (who also lived in Sevorgan at the time) wrinkled her nose in distaste and declared "Ronnie Webb is in here". He was - at the snack bar at the far end of the store, as usual.

Smells - both good and bad - seem to me to be a distinguishing feature of the life of most towns. Falmouth smelled, not unnaturally, of the sea, though the scent which blew up the alleyways on the east wind was often less the fresh, salty tang of the ocean than the slack oily redolence of a busy working harbour, an aroma which, coming from Porthleven, was not entirely unfamiliar to me and which perhaps helped to make me feel at home. Like Porthleven, Falmouth was and is a fishing port, though somehow the little boats tied up to the quays there seemed almost overwhelmed by the looming outlines of the huge tankers further down in the docks themselves.

My father had worked in the docks for a while - one of several jobs he had after the end of the war. The work was both dirty and, at times, dangerous. He did not mind this, but found the atmosphere of the place oppressively claustrophobic, though the pay was good, and he stayed there longer than he might have done for that reason. By the time I was at Tech, however, he had departed to Sunset Farm on the outskirts of Porthleven, where he lovingly tended a small herd of cows and ploughed straight furrows in little pocket-handkerchief-sized fields, and was sublimely happy, though not nearly as well off as the dockers, breathing in fumes from the bilges and avoiding the advances of rats - these latter of uncertain origin, since the ships that came into Falmouth for repair had been in ports all over the world.

Nevertheless, there was an air of romance about it all, especially when some great monster, its refit completed, was towed out on the high tide and with a farewell blast from its great hooter set out again towards the open sea and some destination which might be no more exotic than Southampton, or might, on the other hand, be some far-off island in a blue ocean the like of which we had only ever seen on a screen in the cinema.

It was during that year that I had my own first minor brush with romance. I had never, up to that time, been particularly successful in my relationships with members of the opposite sex - perhaps not surprisingly, since my teenage self was plain, strident and not a little aggressive, though it had been said in my favour that I had fine eyes, a decent figure and exceptionally good legs! None of this, however, had proved sufficient to attract any male approbation in my time at the Grammar School, in an era when if there had been an erogenous zone it would have been the face! I was therefore quite astonished to discover myself the object of the admiration of one of the most handsome-looking day-release boys at the Tech. He did not, it is true, have a very romantic occupation, being a trainee gas-fitter. He came on Fridays and studied whatever it is that gas-fitters have to learn, including welding. The welding shop, for obvious reasons, always had its door standing open and my vanity was flattered when I observed him, as I frequently did, standing with his back to the stream of blue sparks to which he was presumably supposed to be paying attention, gazing out at me as I crossed the yard, with a tender expression on his face. I suppose with hindsight and the cynicism of advancing years, one might call that expression fatuous - but not then. Then it was tender, and he obviously liked me, and I liked him. That, indeed, was about as far as it ever went. Sometimes he made my day by smiling at me, but he was a shy fellow, and seemed almost totally devoid of conversation. On summer afternoons, when the air was heavy with the scent of the buddleia which bloomed in profusion on the still-uncleared bomb-sites in that part of Falmouth, and the sound of the bees would make you feel pleasantly drowsy, we would sit out on the back wall overlooking the docks, eyeing one another silently and pretending to look at the view long past the time when we should have returned to our respective classes. Nothing would be said. Perhaps nothing needed to be said. Eventually, one of us would reluctantly depart indoors to be treated to ribald comment from our peers. It was not, by most people's standards, a very exciting relationship. In retrospect, I am glad of that, for the memory, unsullied by any recollection of embarrassing clinches and fumblings in the back seats of cinemas, or of quarrels occasioned by youthful jealousies, has a degree of perfection about it which could never have been vouchsafed by a more passionate attachment. I still have one photograph of him, taken during that final summer term. I can look at it now with that detached, gentle amusement one feels when contemplating one's own former self - raw and unfinished, perhaps, but possessing that quality of innocence and the unspoiled capacity for wonderment which, long-lost though it may be, was very real at the time and is precious to the memory.

It was all, I suppose, a milestone in my growing-up, and I shall always be grateful to him. Since beginning to write this book, I have been saddened to learn of his death. I had not seen him for many years, yet his passing has left a strange, innocence-shaped gap in my life, which can never be filled.

CHAPTER 3

Life in the Law

IT had never been my intention to work at an ordinary job in an ordinary office in an ordinary town, especially if that town happened to be Helston. I was, I believed at the time, destined for more exciting things. What my exact expectations were, I do not think I really knew myself: suffice it to say that hard reality intruded once again into the dream and caused me to take a more pragmatic view of my situation.

We were all due to leave Tech at the end of July 1951, qualified, so far as that word describes our woeful inadequacies for employment in the real world, to work as typists, secretaries or anything requiring similar skills. At the end of June I still had no job in view: this was a situation little short of critical, given the social climate of the times. Nowadays, half the working population of Cornwall may be unemployed, and whilst protesting noises are justly and frequently made about this deplorable condition, the horrible underlying truth is that technology has become king and his crowning has robbed a large section of the populace of its right to gainful employment. One man (or woman) can do the work which used to need five - the other four find themselves on the scrap heap and must sign on and be grateful. Those who were not around in the 1950s, therefore, may find it difficult to understand that this was not the case then. Being unable to find yourself a job in those days was regarded as something of a disgrace: to be out of work for more than a few weeks branded you as a good-for-nothing wastrel, whilst the long-term unemployed - rightly the recipients of a great deal of sympathy today - were then greatly despised.

So I needed to find a job - any job - just something to tide me over until my great career as I knew not what, took off. I found such a job - and stayed there for fifteen years - not entirely a good advertisement for my initiative and enterprise.

In much the way things were done at that time, I had secured an interview, not from answering a newspaper advert, nor via the Employment Agency, but through the good offices of one Sidney Martin who worked for Mr. Pearce the baker at the end of our road. Sidney, an elderly bachelor, served in the shop, and was always very correctly turned out in black jacket and pinstriped trousers. His manners were quite perfect - perhaps a trifle too perfect for some of Mr. Pearce's cruder customers, who tended not to appreciate refinement in any shape or form, and to mock what they perceived as his self aggrandisement - even though they would not have recognised that phrase if they had heard it. Probably because she decidedly did not come into that category, but was extremely courteous herself, Sidney Martin got on particularly well with my mother and would engage her in conversation whenever she went into the shop. Thus it came about that she mentioned to him that I was due to leave Falmouth Tech and must find myself a job.

"I think" said Sidney after some reflection "I know just the job for Elsie".

He proceeded to "have a word" with a friend of his, one J. Percival Rogers - a well known and highly respected local solicitor, whose firm had offices in Helston and Falmouth. Alas, for my young hopes - there was no vacancy in the Falmouth office; however, it "just so happened" that there was a possible opening for a junior typist in Helston.

Thus it came about that I presented myself one searing hot July day at the offices of Reginald Rogers and Son, 17 Coinagehall Street, Helston, wearing a dress borrowed from my mother because I did not myself possess one I considered suitable for such an august occasion. I was to be interviewed, so I anticipated, by the great Mr. Rogers. Not so! He was in Court that day, and I was seen instead by one of his partners, a stout, silver-haired ex-Army officer named Nott, whom I came to fear and dread, as did every typist in the firm, for his habit of coming back from lunch at about 2.30 pm, dictating for at least an hour and a half, and then requiring all his work to be typed for dispatch that same day! He was, I regret to say, a quite impossible boss - however, at my interview he confined himself to examining my dubious skills by dictating two short letters and sending me down to type them. Nerves rendered my none-too-expert fingers akin to the proverbial bunch of bananas, and I made several errors before completing this necessary test of my abilities. The problem was compounded for me by the fact that I was required to take two carbon copies (I had never taken more than one before, and that only infrequently!) This, of course, was in the days when correcting fluid was unheard of; much less correcting keys - all mistakes had to be rubbed out, and often the result of this was a dirty black smudge, and the need to re-type the whole thing.

Mr. Nott, however, seemed reasonably satisfied with my performance and I flushed with pleasure when, after his inspection of my exam results, he declared, "You got a jolly good School Cert." The job was mine: I was to start work the following Monday.

School leavers - particularly those who have had technical training for the jobs they occupy - tend to think they know it all and will set their employers' firms by the ears. I was quickly made to realise that this was not to be the case. Far from knowing everything, I knew nothing. My first weeks passed in a confusing blur of being asked to perform tasks which, once learned, would be simple, but at the outset seemed totally incomprehensible. Even operating the telephone was far from straightforward. We had, at that stage, two lines to the exchange, with extensions to the various rooms in that large, rambling building in which we worked. The system was operated from an ancient switchboard which was, to me, truly appalling in its complexity. This evil mechanism was contained in a large polished wooden box, about three feet wide by two feet high, and about a foot deep. It stood on the counter in the reception area. At the top of its workface was a long row of what looked like eyelids: below these were three rows of little levers. To this day I am uncertain what function was served by the middle row! As to the rest, to get an outside line you pressed the top lever below the appropriate eyelid and waited for the operator to ask for the required number. When you had been connected, you had to suspend the call by flicking the bottom lever upwards whilst you got through to the appropriate extension inside the office. This you did by pressing the lever under the eyelid for that extension, and turning a large handle on the end of the box. The eyelid would blink rapidly until the occupant of the room answered his telephone. In principle, the rest was easy; you informed him that his call was waiting, flicked the lever on the exchange line back into place and hey presto! he was connected! Or should have been. It was devilishly easy to cut the caller off by flicking the wrong switch, or turning it in the wrong direction, or putting the receiver down too soon. Then the whole miserable process had to be started again.

It was particularly dreadful if you were making a call to Mawnan Smith, which you often did (a) because several very important clients lived there and (b) because it was the home of one of the firm's partners, and he would wish to telephone his wife. To reach Mawnan Smith you had to go through the Helston Exchange which was situated in Wendron Street and employed quite a number of local people. They would connect you to the Falmouth Exchange, who would connect you, hopefully, to the Mawnan Smith Exchange. You never knew when or whether you might actually get through. You would hear the voice of the Falmouth operator saying "Falmouth, Falmouth"...then the Helston operator would request "Mawnan Smith......Mawnan......Smith" , then, again "Falmouth.......Mawnan Smith" and eventually, if you were lucky, the operator in Mawnan Smith itself would request the number. If, having gone through all this, you then lost the call by pressing the wrong lever, the frustration you felt was more than appreciable.

Eventually, as one does, I came to terms with the lethal instrument. There were many other processes to be mastered, however, some of them simple, others more difficult. Some seemed, even in those days, just a little antiquated -the Letter Book, for instance. I have come across no office in the last thirty five years which kept a Letter Book, but they were commonly used by firms in the 1940s and early 50s, mostly as a back-up to shaky filing systems. The idea was that each outgoing letter had two carbon copies - one white, one coloured. The white one went into the client's file whilst the coloured one went into the Letter Book, and was given a number, which was then recorded in an alphabetical index. At busy times, when there was a lot of correspondence going out, this tedious daily task could easily consume most of one person's morning. As a system, however, it had its merits, since it was often easier to use the Letter Book to trace information than to locate the file itself, which might be lurking in any one of three or four people's rooms, or even in transit between them.

The filing system itself was also somewhat Dickensian. To begin with, there were no cabinets: all files were stored in what passed for alphabetical order on open shelves in one room, which contained a vast table. Every morning the filing baskets from the clerks' and partners' rooms were emptied and their contents dumped on this table for sorting into bundles - again alphabetically. We were each in charge of sections for filing - mine was A to H for as long as I can remember. "Doing the filing" could take anything from fifteen minutes to an hour, provided you were not interrupted, but as often as not someone would want to dictate letters, or a document would be in urgent need of engrossment because the client was coming in at 10 am to sign it, and you had to leave the filing where it was and return later, usually to find that your carefully sorted bundles had been raided by someone and scattered all over the table, so you had to start all over again. It was a kind of Augean stable: I never remember a single day when that table was absolutely cleared.

I was not often called upon, in those early months, to tackle the engrossing of deeds, and I have to admit that this was a matter of some relief to me. Computers have made engrossing easy; mistakes can simply be cancelled on screen and corrected, and the final print-out thus rendered perfect. Not so in 1951! Perfection was still the required standard; unfortunately it was not, at that point of time, the standard of my typing.

Hand engrossing was still fashionable in those days and was much sought after for the really important document, so that the finished result would look impressive even before it was read. In our firm, hand-engrossing was done by Kenneth (known as Kenny) Wearne, who was a superb calligrapher. I liked Kenny. He was a kind friend and mentor, and I regarded him as my particular ally amongst the senior staff. He was also very amusing: he spent a great deal of his time in the Courts, and would come back full of interesting and exciting tales of who had said what and how long a sentence had been handed out.

People you worked with long ago tend to have a habit of walking in procession through your mind. I do not even need to close my eyes to see those colleagues of my early working life. There was Douglas (Dougie) Charles, the firm's book-keeper. He was the eldest of the clerks - all of thirty - and had fought in North Africa during the war. I regarded him as middle-aged and was foolish enough, on one occasion, to say so: this gave him great offence, something I can understand now, but could not, for the life of me, comprehend then. A quiet, sensible type of man, Dougie had one great weakness - he made constant use of the word "bloody" - to the extent that we dubbed him "Bloody Charles" although no-one ever called him that to his face.

Jack Pryor, the managing clerk, was a great favourite with elderly widows, who tended to fall for his boyish good looks and made frequent appointments to see him about their imagined legal problems. Jack's war had taken place mainly in the English Channel, where he seemed to have spent a great deal of time dashing around on short but dangerous missions with the Navy. I suspect that he found civilian life dull by comparison, for he easily became frustrated by office routine. He had a good brain and an excellent grasp of legal complexities, but he also tended to run on a somewhat short fuse at times, resulting in numerous arguments and shouting matches round the office when anyone was unwise enough to disagree with him on an off-day. The storm, however, would soon pass and the comfortable atmosphere in which the firm usually operated would be restored.

Ronnie Rosewarne I already knew well; he lived in the next road to us in Porthleven. At the time I started work he was away recuperating after a near-fatal motor-cycle accident, from which he eventually made a good recovery. He took over the firm's book-keeping when Bloody Charles was transferred to Falmouth office, and was best known for his neat, meticulous approach to everything. He would pore over every typed letter which arrived on his desk, muttering "typing error there...spelling mistake there....." then he would pull a wry face and make corrections in ink which, if they were sufficient in number (i.e. more than one small one) would necessitate a re-type on the part of the unfortunate typist concerned. He never caught me out in a spelling mistake, but alas, numerous typing errors were exposed in those early days.

RR's other strength was his dry sense of humour. He had the happy knack of being able to turn most situations into a joke - a valuable attribute in any workplace, especially one where pressure - and tempers - could run rather high at times.

Then there was "Boy Ray". Raymond was always known as "Boy Ray" so long as he worked for the firm, which he did for many years, starting as an office boy at the age of fourteen and becoming senior litigation clerk before departing to run the Magistrates' Court office at Penryn. When I first joined Rogers and Son, Boy Ray occupied some mediocre middle stratum in the system, which necessitated his undertaking some quite complicated tasks on the one hand and totally menial ones on the other. It must have been a confusing life. He was, for instance, in charge of insurances and held high-powered conferences with loss adjusters - he controlled the strongroom, which he ruled with a rod of iron - but he was also responsible for stoking the coke-fired boiler on winter evenings. For this he required an assistant to help him shovel the coke from its hole under the stairs and carry it to the boiler room. Marilyn, my co-junior and I would take turns to carry out this loathsome task. You became quite filthy and in addition missed the 5.15 bus home and had to wait about to catch one of the workmen's buses around 6 o'clock.

There were two such buses. One brought workmen in from Culdrose and the other came from Falmouth Docks. The Culdrose bus was definitely the livelier of the two - partly because the dock workers had left home at 6.30 am and were mostly asleep by the time their home-coming bus reached Helston. Several Porthleven men worked in the docks at that time - quite a percentage of them seemed to have the same surname - Gilbert. One was Boy Ray's father, George Gilbert - another was Harry Gilbert, known as Harry Gibby - and yet another was Stanley Gilbert, known as Stumpy, not for any physical defect, but because of the title of a dreadful Victorian ballad he had once sung in a long-ago concert "Poor Stumpy little boy...". These three Gilberts were not closely related to each other, but the name was common in both Porthleven and Helston: indeed, at a slightly later date we had a partner in the firm who was also called Gilbert.

The Culdrose bus was quite different from the dockers'. The men travelling on it sang hymns, a phenomenon brought about by the presence of one Jim Miners, an elderly and most lovable man, a Methodist

Local Preacher of many years' standing and a kind friend to our entire village. Jim was boss on the Culdrose bus: he would brook no bad language and no arguments. To eliminate the possibility of these, he would strike up a hymn as soon as he had boarded the bus: his fellow-passengers would join in and by the time they reached Helston a fine choral performance was going on.

Singing was, as I recall, an integral part of life in those days. We even sang in the office, though it cannot be claimed that this was common practice throughout the legal profession in Helston: it was one of the eccentricities for which the staff of Rogers and Son were well-known. But sing we did. Boy Ray was a fine tenor, who competed in music festivals throughout the county and often brought home awards: Ronnie was an excellent bass. Margaret had a good clear soprano, and I could manage the alto part if I had learned it, or something which harmonised and passed for alto if I had not. Singing was a favourite pastime when we were doing the filing in the mornings, although our efforts were not always entirely appreciated by those trying to work upstairs, as the sound of our voices floated upwards. Jack, who was tone deaf in any case, really hated us to sing. I also well remember one day when one of the firm's partners came down and suggested in a pained voice that perhaps we "might have a little rest from singing...we've had a piece of Handel, a piece of Mendelssohn; songs from the shows and various hymns - surely enough is enough!" We acceded to his request, of course; indeed, we had no option but to do so, but next morning in his absence we were trilling away again quite happily. People nowadays do not, as a rule, sing whilst working - and the world is the poorer for it. Tinned rubbish played on transistor radios - or worse, amplified so that there is no avoiding it if you are within several hundred yards - is no substitute for the exercise of the human voice, however feeble. Singing releases the spirit and liberates the soul when one is doing some otherwise mundane and boring task.

Mr. Price, - he who asked us to stop singing that morning - was an extraordinary man. Not everyone warmed to him, but I did. He was long, lean and saturnine, and affected a highly individual style of clothing. Almost always a cavalry twill suit; a navy-blue spotted bow tie and, in the street, a broad-brimmed brown hat rather like those worn by trainers on race days. He drove a Morris Traveller - and when a new car was needful, he bought another Morris Traveller, with which, despite being extremely well off (he had a private fortune from a deceased aunt) he seemed always to be entirely satisfied. His wife, an accomplished musician, was a cellist; they had no children but appeared deeply content with each other: their many interests included, of course, music (despite, or perhaps allied to, the request to us to stop singing) and they were both keen gardeners.

OFP, as we called him should, I think, have been a theatre manager rather than a lawyer. Indeed it was whispered down the grapevine from Falmouth Office that he spent a great deal of time in the Polytechnic Hall, putting out the chairs for forthcoming concerts. He was in fact President of the Falmouth Polytechnic Society for a number of years.

Oliver Price's war was something of a mystery. Nearly every male member of the firm (with the exception of Mr. Rogers, who was too old, and Boy Ray, who was too young) had been in the forces during World War II. OFP had served in the Navy, but it was generally noted with some scorn that he had spent most of his time "out in Mexico" where of course there had been no great action! I became intrigued by this, developed my own theory about it, and one day plucked up the courage to ask him "Sir, were you a spy in the war?" His answer was typically understated. "We...ll, not exactly a spy... I suppose.....yes, I was in Intelligence. We had to sit on the cliffs in Mexico and intercept radio messages from enemy shipping.....the problem was that we were usually about a fortnight behind with the de-coding...." He raised one eyebrow. No more was said. No more needed to be said.

Another of OFP's tasks - he being at that time the junior partner in the firm - was to impart to members of staff the good or bad news regarding their annual rises. Perhaps it should be explained that solicitors in those days (in Helston at any rate: I cannot vouch for other towns) were notoriously bad payers, a rule to which Rogers and Son was regrettably no exception. My own starting rate was two pounds ten shillings per week, rising annually by five shillings a week until, after some few years, I rebelled and demanded a rise of at least one pound. They gave me fifteen shillings! In the early days, however, after deductions for my keep at home, bus fares to work, lunches etc, I was left with spending power in the region of seven shillings and sixpence, which I suppose was better than nothing. Employees with family responsibilities, however, often had a really hard time surviving upon the pittances they received each week, and we all grumbled constantly about our ill-paid states.

Because we were constantly short of money we were always delighted when there was a General Election, because this meant that we could forsake the office for a day to fill the relatively lucrative posts of poll clerks in the various villages of the constituency. My own first experience of this was at St. Keverne, where I had to arrive at 7 am. I have no recollection at all of how I got there: presumably several of us shared a taxi, but I was never at my best before 10 am and simply cannot remember.

It turned out to be a pouring wet day. The Conservative tellers, outside the school gates, had arrived equipped with a large van in which to sit. Halfway through the morning they took pity on their Labour and Liberal counterparts, who all piled in with them, and formed one jolly party for the rest of the time. Meanwhile, the Police arrived with the news that there "was trouble down Gunwalloe". Apparently the person appointed to preside at the election had misunderstood his instructions and gone to Baripper (near Camborne) instead of Berepper (at Gunwalloe). Unfortunately he had chosen a bicycle as his preferred method of transport and at mid-morning had been seen pedalling furiously through Nancegollan! Presumably he did eventually arrive and presumably the voters of Gunwalloe were able to cast their votes in the time-honoured tradition.

The day was long and not a little tedious; vast quantities of tea were consumed in the polling station at St. Keverne, as no doubt they were in others throughout the land, and our stock of sandwiches and buns seemed to run out very early. Even so, coming back across Goonhilly Downs in the early summer dusk (the rain had gone off by then) with the sealed ballot box bouncing wildly on the back seat of the Presiding Officer's car, I suddenly had a sense of being part of something very important; very precious. I lived in a country where people could choose their Government: where things were done honestly and properly and with due decorum. Extra money or no extra money, it had been a day well spent.

The financial euphoria resulting from the election was, however, short-lived, and we soon resumed our normal pattern of fiscal anxiety.

On one occasion, somewhere around the end of the Tax Year, Boy Ray went into Mr. Price's office for some reason. OFP was studying the end-of-year tax returns. There was, at the time, a considerable national scandal about the amount of money required to fund the ill-fated Blue Streak rocket project. Looking up from his task, OFP drawled "I say, Raymond, you don't seem to have made much of a contribution to Blue Streak!" Boy Ray was infuriated - it was one of the very few occasions I ever saw him out of humour. "If I got more money I'd pay more tax" he snarled on his return to the general office. But he was teased about Blue Streak for years afterwards.

When I remember the partners at Rogers and Son I am amazed at the strong definition of their characters. They were not, as is commonly supposed by the public when it thinks of the legal profession "faceless men in grey suits" - indeed, I can rarely remember any one of them ever wearing a grey suit - but what I do remember is how vastly different they were from each other, and what strong impacts they variously made on the lives of those of us who worked for them Mr. Nott, for instance, was what nowadays might be termed a high flyer. He had a glamorous wife and two good-looking children; he was involved with various business ventures outside his legal practice and it was said of him that he "sailed close to the wind". I was not quite sure what was meant by that phrase, and would not like to comment now, though he certainly had some very colourful friends and acquaintances who would call at the office to see him. Some of these were extremely pleasant people; others less so.

One in particular, another ex-army man called Captain Pinfield, used to strike fear and terror into the reception staff whenever he entered the premises. He was the sort of man who barked at you rather than making any attempt at normal conversation; indeed, snapped commands seemed to be his only means of communication. We all longed for him to be taken down a peg, but never supposed that it would be Beth, our new office junior, who would accomplish that miracle. Beth was very new and very nervous; she had never met Captain Pinfield before when he came in one day demanding to see Mr. Nott immediately. "What name please?" enquired Beth timidly. "Pinfield" he snarled between his teeth, obviously insulted that there should be anyone permitted to be in the firm at all who did not know him. Beth meekly dialled Mr. Nott's room. "Captain Pinhead is here to see you, sir". Great was our hilarity, whilst "Pinhead's" face grew purple with rage. The mistake was rectified and an apology dutifully made - but the damage was done. "Pinhead" he remained and I am sure he was well aware of the fact, for he always pronounced his name with great care if ever he was asked for it again.

Beth had another major disaster in her early days with the firm. Mr. Rogers had a peculiar habit of dictating during lunch, which was always brought up to him on a tray from the Brown Owl tearooms just down the road. No-one particularly liked having to fetch the tray, so it usually fell to the junior's lot. On this occasion, Beth had been kept waiting rather a long time in the kitchen of the Brown Owl, and was hurrying up the stairs with the loaded tray. The plates of food, as usual, were covered by inverted dishes, with a cloth placed over the whole. As she reached the top step, Beth tripped and lost her footing. It would have been bad enough had Mr. Rogers himself not been coming along the landing at that precise moment, to be greeted by a dish of prunes and custard flying through the air towards him, followed up by a hail of vegetables and gravy! Fortunately he was the kindest of men, and expressed more concern for Beth's person than for the lost lunch - which was of course replaced at extra cost to himself.

Mr. Rogers - or JPR as we thought of him - was the sort of man who ought perhaps to have a whole book written about him, not merely part of a chapter. He belonged, quite frankly, to another age, and never seemed entirely at ease in the post-war world, though he was tough enough to cope with it. He remained a bachelor almost to the end of his life - certainly at the time of which we are talking he had no notion of ever marrying anyone. He was well connected, being on his father's side a relative of Captain Lionel Rogers, the then squire of Penrose: his mother belonged to a branch of the Fox family, who owned various estates in the Falmouth area, including the famous Glendurgan. JPR himself was, by most people's standards, immensely rich, owning a large number of farms in the Liskeard and Launceston areas - where he perpetuated the ancient custom of a half-yearly Rent Court. He would stay at The White Hart, Launceston, for a couple of days and meet his tenants to discuss their problems and receive his dues. His private life appeared to be very simple and centred mainly around the church. He lived with an elderly aunt whom I never met, and who was always referred to as "Aunt Fan". There was, for a while, another aunt "Aunt Bob" who presumably died, because she faded out of the story quite early on.

JPR had not, however, spent the whole of his life in the company of elderly ladies. He had served in the Army in World War I: he always kept in touch with his batman and sent him a present every year at Christmas.

We had, when I was supposed to be taking dictation, many interesting conversations about religion. He was a committed Anglo Catholic, and constantly challenged my rather unquestioning and traditional Methodist stance on various issues. Indeed, we would argue quite fiercely at times, but we found much common ground, and whilst I always fought my non-conformist corner, I secretly appreciated being enlightened on the viewpoint of someone from a Christian tradition so very different from the one in which I had grown up.

On any subject, JPR was a remarkably easy person to talk to - this despite the fact that he was quite a few years older than my own father and was, in addition, my ultimate superior in the workplace. This rapport may have stemmed partly from the fact that our first-ever conversation occurred without my knowing who he was - thus liberating me from the usual tension and shyness of the new office junior in the presence of "the boss". It also helped that the conversation in question took place, not in the office at all, but on a boat in the middle of the river Fal. It was the occasion of the annual office outing, to which I had been invited in spite of only having been employed in the firm for the space of a week! A boat had been chartered for the trip up river and back down to Percuil and St. Mawes. Mr. Nott, supposedly in charge of this gentle expedition, managed to navigate us on to a mudbank in the ebbing tide: we only escaped with a great deal of sweating and swearing and leaping about in dinghies and hauling on ropes.

Other than this, the trip was very pleasant: the day was warm and still; the atmosphere relaxed. Enjoying myself immensely, and feeling extremely grown-up and liberated, I leaned on the rail and chatted amiably to the "elderly gentleman" next to me. He, in turn, pointed out places of interest along the banks and appeared to be very knowledgeable about such people as Lord Falmouth. On disembarking for lunch, I enquired of Marilyn who my companion might be. In an awed whisper she informed me that he was no less a person than JPR himself.

First impressions being what they are, the inevitable consequence of this encounter was that although I always respected JPR I could never be intimidated by him. To be fair, he was not a frightening person, though he could assert his authority when necessary and on occasions could become quite angry about certain bêtes noir. He would, for instance, stump around the office inspecting various people's rooms, and woe betide anyone who had a clutter of filing - or worse still, deeds lying about. "Dumps!" he would exclaim wrathfully "I will not have dumps! Most of the time, however, he was kindly and concerned about everyone, if perhaps just a little detached from the levels at which we lived our lives and consequently not always comprehending our problems - particularly financial ones. I found him great fun, and regarded him as a friend. Since he was generally considered to be something of a misogynist, I suppose this was rather an achievement on my part, though I am inclined to believe the misogyny was a label unfairly stuck on him. To me he was always charming - more like an eccentric elderly uncle than an employer whom I needed to please or impress.

JPR was what used to be called "a man of parts". When I joined the firm he was engaged upon the publication in book form of a series of monographs on the Cornish saints, written by his erudite friend, the late Canon Doble, one time Vicar of Wendron. The work eventually came out, not without a considerable struggle, in several large volumes, Canon Doble's knowledge of his subject having been extensive to say the least. You seldom took dictation from JPR at that time without at least one lengthy letter going off to the publishers on the subject of Canon Doble and the Cornish Saints.

Amongst his other accomplishments, JPR was a Fellow of the Royal Genealogical Society, and as such received many enquiries from people about their family trees. It is rather difficult to explain on paper and at this space of time, why we should have found the names of people's ancestors so hilariously funny, but I can remember occasions when both of us were almost helpless with mirth as he dictated the details of some pedigree and we tried to envisage the possible characters of long dead people with improbable names.

Many of the applicants for genealogical information were Mormons - who now much prefer to be referred to as Latter Day Saints. Because members of this sect practise baptism for the dead, they always had - and indeed still have - a massive interest in their family histories. JPR would be much impressed, I am sure, to see the huge computerised records kept by the Latter Day Saints in Helston today - a facility of which we are all glad to make frequent use. In those days, of course, there was no Mormon church in the town, and most of JPR's requests for information came straight from Salt Lake City, Utah. I particularly remember one Doctor Alton I. Moyle, who seemed to write in every other week requesting information on this and that long-dead relative.

One of the most interesting of all the pedigrees had nothing at all to do with the Mormons. It was that of the Hammill family, well-known in Porthleven - indeed, I had attended junior school with Loveday Hammill, who was a little older than me. It was intriguing to learn that this family were descended from the Comtes d'Hamel in eleventh century France - more so that they, in turn, had descended from the Kings of Denmark in the year eight hundred and something. Now they were a nice ordinary family living in my home village. Sic transit gloria!

During the war, JPR had acted as Town Clerk of Helston, in addition to running his private law practices in Helston and Falmouth. To accomplish this with any degree of efficiency, he had to work very long hours indeed, often well into the night. It was on such an occasion, he told me, that he had encountered the office ghost.

Working late in his room at 17 Coinagehall Street on a winter night, he had heard footsteps ascending the stairs. He had felt no apprehension; indeed, hoping it was one of the clerks, he had gone to the door to ask whoever it was to fetch a file for him. There was no-one on the stairs - but the footsteps kept coming - and coming. They passed him and went on through the wall - presumably into Barclays Bank next door! JPR packed up and went home early that night.

That the building was supposed to be haunted was an accepted fact among the staff. Indeed, I had a strange and inexplicable experience there myself one summer afternoon. I had been to early lunch and returned at 1 pm, when the building was largely deserted. I saw a man, whom I took to be Boy Ray, come down the back stairs and go into the typists' room. I needed some information from Raymond, so I hurried after him. The room was empty. Soundless. There was no-one there - and those who worked with me at the time can vouch for the fact that in that room there was nowhere anyone could have hidden. Raymond, as I might have known, had gone home to lunch at one o'clock.

The lunch hour, and the manner of spending it, varied considerably from person to person throughout the firm. I normally met my friend Sylvia, who was working for a local firm of estate agents, and we would eat sandwiches in the Coronation park, which was very pleasant on a sunny day: less so if you had to cower in one of the shelters to escape the rain. It had the merit, however, of saving expense: quite frankly we could not afford to eat in cafes very often. Amongst the better-off, the favourite lunchtime venue was the Brown Owl, a stylish little place just down the road from the office, run by two spinster ladies, Miss Pawlyn and Miss Wyatt. The former was quite a character; always a rather hearty type, she had played hockey for Cornwall in her time and remained very sporty well into her old age, being a keen golfer. She had a reputation as something of a tough nut, and it has to be admitted that at times her language could be somewhat colourful.   Miss Wyatt was probably the perfect foil to Miss Pawlyn: also a golfer, but much less formidable; extremely refined and ladylike.   Together they made an excellent team and ran a popular and thriving business.   The Brown Owl was a charming and delightful place, furnished with comfortable wickerwork chairs and little glass-topped tables with wickerwork legs. In spite of the boisterous Miss Pawlyn, its ambience was sedate - olde worlde, even, and it was a favourite place for tea, coffee and lunch, in connection with which it forms the backdrop to one of the most hilarious incidents to occur during my time at Rogers and Son.

About noon one day, our Mr. Patterson was interviewing a couple of clients, and needed their deeds from the strongroom.   Leaving his visitors sitting comfortably in his office, he went downstairs to fetch the said deeds, which proved harder to locate than he had supposed.   He was interrupted in his search by a couple of incoming telephone calls, which distracted him somewhat from the task in hand.   Then he noticed the time.   It was well past his lunch hour and he was hungry.   Totally forgetting the two clients waiting patiently in his room, he sailed down to the Brown Owl and ordered roast beef, into which he was tucking with some relish when to his intense embarrassment and horror, his two somewhat bewildered-looking clients walked in, having decided to abandon their long wait in his office and take their own lunch break.

Mr. Patterson (known, like the rest of the partners, by his initials, JLP) was notably absent-minded, a trait related to the fact that he carried an almost impossibly large workload, some of which could and should have been dealt with by other, less energetic and dedicated members of staff.   His desk was always deep in files and draft documents, the latter mostly written out in his own execrable handwriting: like many professional people, he paid little attention to legibility. However, because he suffered from a stutter, he understandably preferred writing things out to dictating, though the consequence for the typing department was often a missed bus in the evenings, as he would come hurtling down the stairs at the very last minute with a handful of scribbles, requiring "just one more" letter to go off urgently in that evening's post.

Urgency was the norm in all departments. Everything seemed to have a deadline - even straightforward conveyancing often carried a barely achievable time-limit. We had a saying to the effect that clients' purchases had to be completed "as soon as possible or earlier by arrangement".

The occasions of real panic, however, would occur when a big case was coming up for trial in Court. It need not necessarily be an exciting case, and indeed, most cases were not. Nevertheless, a deadly dull civil action could still engender quite a frenzy of activity around the place. I well recall one particular occasion when a client of ours - a cattle-feed merchant by occupation - had brought proceedings against a farmer customer of his, relating to allegedly unpaid bills - a routine enough matter, one might have supposed, but the case was defended and the whole thing escalated to such proportions that learned Counsel were instructed on both sides and huge briefs, with masses of accompanying documentary evidence, had to be prepared at rather short notice.

The day before the hearing, our typing room floor was literally strewn, almost ankle deep in places, with copies of old accounts and letters going back, it seemed, for years; innumerable pages of brief and other cardinal necessities of getting the case into Court the next morning. Adrenalin ran high on occasions like this: the effect was to translate the mundane into the exciting. You felt part of something that was extremely important; winning or losing might depend upon your speed and accuracy; you became aware that the firm's reputation hung, not merely upon Counsel's performance in Court, but upon your ability to furnish him with the documentary ammunition he needed. Everything hinged upon what you and others were doing in the background. In fact, you were necessary to the whole process of justice, and the knowledge of this was exhilarating and perhaps a little frightening. It certainly taught you to work under pressure, and thus formed a vital factor in your growing up. There came an awareness that you were no longer merely rehearsing for life and its demands and experiences: you were involved in the real thing: a necessary part of the whole. The result was that like a butterfly coming out of its chrysalis, you flexed the wings of your new found competence and felt you could take on the world.

CHAPTER 4

Home and Leisure

"THE Gue, Porthleven" was not considered a prestigious address. Its main claim to fame was - and is - that of being one of the steepest roads in the entire village, plunging wildly down at an angle of something approaching one in four, for all the world like some primeval fairground ride. Indeed, the more daring spirits amongst the local boys liked to use it in much that way, racing down the alarming gradient in "butts" - soapboxes on wheels, steered by pieces of rope connected to crude front axles. These precarious vehicles tended to gather speed as they went - spills were frequent and damage to limbs not unknown.

The buildings in The Gue are an assortment of unconnected architectural styles - and indeed in some cases of no style whatsoever. Near the top of the hill stand granite-fronted detached and semi-detached houses, solid, respectable-looking dwellings of which their original Victorian owners were doubtless justly proud. Sadly, their once-pretty front gardens have largely gone, making way for parking spaces, but I remember them crammed with roses, pinks and other summer flowers. Further down the hill you come upon a collection of cottages, most of them now renovated beyond recognition, but still lying higgledy piggledy amongst each other, some facing the road - others squeezed in at the back and reached via unmade "openings" - alleyways between the houses in front.

In one such cottage my parents and I lived for upwards of twenty years, just four doors down from my close friend Mabel and only a short way up from the yard where Joe Ching had his granite works. Joe was a Monumental Mason of some distinction, as were his forbears and indeed, his son, Jack, who followed him in the business. I had grown up beside Ching's works, and in childhood took no notice at all of the assortment of headstones in various stages of completion which littered the place. These memorials to the dead were a part of everyday life to us, and by no means to be regarded as gruesome. Ching's, however, was a constant source of irritation to the occupants of nearby dwellings, on account of the fact that its largely unsuppressed drilling machinery tended to interfere with radio reception, often at peak listening times, since the Chings, friendly people and amongst the best of neighbours, nonetheless had little sense of timing, and if they were running up against a deadline they would drill away at all hours of the day and often well into the night.

George Ching, one of Joe's sons, ran a car repair business next door to his father's works. George enjoyed a very high reputation as a mechanic, but conducted his working affairs in a somewhat haphazard manner, with vehicles in various stages of repair spread up and down the road with a blithe disregard of neatness and order. One of the consequences of this was that it was no new thing to have to step over George's feet, protruding from under a car, as you passed the place where he was working. "Morning George" you would say and "Morning" a disembodied voice would reply from beneath the vehicle. Sometimes the voice would belong to George - sometimes to his mate, Philip Taylor, who worked with him. I lived in the same road as Philip for years, but cannot really remember him in any other connection than that of mechanic; indeed I rarely recall seeing him dressed in anything but an extremely oily boiler suit, wriggling out from beneath some elderly Ford or Morris, clutching a spanner and grinning toothily out of a face covered in grime.

The Gue was a community in the way that streets nowadays are not. This had both advantages and disadvantages, disrespect for privacy being one of the latter. Neighbours tended to barge into your house without knocking and interrupt whatever happened to be going on in order to give you the latest piece of gossip, or to borrow a cup of sugar, or merely to tell you how exhausted they were after their day's work. "Just killed" was the favourite phrase in that connection. No matter that you were eating your dinner, or listening to your favourite radio programme, or trying to read a book or write a letter, or wash your hair - they had arrived "just killed" and you must needs pay attention. In return you had their entire support. You could turn to any one of them for any help it was within their power to give. Small gifts - chiefly of food - were constantly being exchanged. Fishermen would bring you a few crab claws or a nice mackerel. In return, my father would take their wives some tomatoes or a cucumber from his greenhouse, or a bunch of Sweet William, supposedly grown for sale to supplement his wages, but in actual fact bestowed liberally upon friends and neighbours. That was the way of The Gue. If something was broken there was always someone who would come and repair it, usually free of charge. If someone was sick or dying, the local women would be there, helping to tend the patient and support the family. My own mother did quite a lot of this sort of thing and was never in the least afraid of exposure to infection. "God will look after me" she would declare - and indeed, I never remember her ever becoming ill as a result of her many forays into sickrooms.

Nonetheless, as I grew up I began to find The Gue increasingly claustrophobic, though I remained fiercely loyal to all our friends and neighbours there, with many of whom I still have close relationships, maintained over the years. But with all the arrogance of early youth and an embryonic snobbery comparable to that of the Old-Woman-in-the-Vinegar-Bottle, I longed to live in a bigger and better house. Gibson Way would have done nicely. This not unattractive crescent of Council dwellings was named after Guy Gibson, leader of the Dam-Busters raid, who spent part of his childhood and early youth in Porthleven at the home of his grandparents and was regarded as an "honorary Porthlevener". The crescent was erected on the outskirts of the village just after the war. The houses there boasted proper damp courses, comfortable living space and the ultimate luxury of modern bathrooms! Those families fortunate enough to be allocated one of these dream palaces - officially opened by Aneurin Bevan himself, then Minister for Housing - were the envy of most of the village. Alas, we were not numbered among them and had to content ourselves in The Gue for a few years longer.

The better-off element of the population, however, tended to live in owner-occupied houses or bungalows in Torleven Road, known colloquially as "Preacher's Lane" on account of the Methodist Manse at the far end. They also lived on Harbour View - invariably referred to as "Breageside" or Unity Road, derisively nicknamed "Piano Street" because of the musical ambitions entertained by the mothers there for their largely untalented offspring.

72

You could walk up the Unity at almost any time of the day or night and listen to indifferent renderings of "The Bluebells of Scotland" or "My Bonnie lies over the ocean" or, if the victim was feeling really rebellious, and mother was out of earshot, "Chopsticks". A few of these not-very-promising beginners eventually became competent, some by virtue of ability and others by sheer dogged persistence. For myself, I had always envied them their opportunities, denied to me both by the absence of an instrument upon which to practise, and the money to pay for lessons - a lethal combination of circumstances so far as any ideas of breaking into the musical world were concerned.

My father played the piano by ear, and if ever he had the chance he would sit down and produce complicated tunes, sometimes with variations, using both hands quite happily as though he had been born with some special knowledge - as indeed I often wondered if he had, for the best I could ever manage was "The First Noel" picked out with one finger and laboriously learned in odd moments in other people's sitting rooms.

The piano was still the most fashionable of musical instruments, though it was soon to suffer at least a partial eclipse with the arrival of the electric guitar and rock 'n roll. Had they known this, its half-hearted exponents in Unity Road would probably have practised with even less dedication. But the piano was still necessary to quite a number of our leisure activities, in particular the phenomena known as "the Socials" at which the hapless pianist spent the entire evening chained to the instrument, churning out all the jolly tunes necessary to the event.

The social calendar for the autumn and winter tended to revolve around "the Socials". These simple but convivial gatherings were so stylised that they deserve some detailed description. They usually took place either in one of the two Methodist Sunday Schools or in the

Public Hall. In the latter venue, some dancing would be included, but not in the Sunday School rooms. Dancing was frowned upon by our elders and betters - presumably because it involved being held in the embrace of a member of the opposite sex and might lead to sinful carryings-on! The taboo, however, was easily overcome by the inclusion of games of "Oyster Sir" and "Three Jolly Fishermen" - both versions of "Kiss-in-the-ring" - and the kissing would be sustained and prolonged in some instances. To be chosen as a partner in "Oyster Sir" by someone you liked and admired was the high spot of the evening - only surpassed if the same person selected you as his partner for "A Hunting We Will Go" - another perfect excuse for lingering embraces, and probably the prelude to being taken home by the favoured one. All this, of course, had a reverse side to it: you might be selected - and in my experience often were - by someone for whose attentions you felt no inclination whatsoever; the result was that you would then spend the remainder of the evening avoiding him, and would have to rush away in a hurry at the end to avoid his offer to escort you home, with all the horrid possibilities that might entail!

"The Socials" however, were not merely the prerogative of the young and single. Plenty of middle-aged couples attended and enjoyed them. There was usually a huge "faith supper" to which everyone brought a contribution. This hit-or-miss method of catering normally worked out very well, though I remember one evening when it did not. The Youth Club were holding a social and I was helping in the kitchen beforehand. Phyllis Arthur, one of my co-workers, surveyed a barely believable array of Swiss rolls spread out on the worktop, and observed "If one more Swiss roll arrives, we shall all be yodelling!" The strange thing, however, was not that this sort of situation occurred, but that it so rarely did. The normal faith supper would, without any prior planning, usually turn out to be an excellent mix of sandwiches, cakes and other dainties, which disappeared like snow before the sun in the face of the hearty appetites of healthy young men.

The season of the Socials began in September, with the "Opening Social" of the Youth Club's winter session. There was usually then a lull until December, when Socials appeared thick and fast in a crowded calendar, and continued to do so throughout the festive season. The Youth Club Christmas party: the Peverell Road Choir Social; the Fore Street Choir Social....and of course, the really big one, the New Year's Eve Social. This particular event was distinguished by being permitted to continue till eleven o'clock instead of the usual ten-thirty deadline! We happily then adjusted our mood and attended the Watchnight Service at eleven-fifteen, after which, wrapped up in heavy coats and woollen scarves, we would arm ourselves with saucepan lids and tin cans, and make noisy progress round the town, on the pretext of wishing people a Happy New Year - no doubt most of them would have been much happier without our deafening greetings.

The Youth Club also held a formal dinner once a year at the end of January. We did all the catering ourselves with very inadequate facilities, but the meal was nonetheless well worth the eating. The church ministers and other dignitaries would be invited: speeches would be made. Afterwards, however, when the tables had been cleared away, the evening became yet another "Social" with Oyster Sir and Hunting We Will Go prominent on the menu. Indeed, apart from the food, the only thing which distinguished the evening from the other Socials was the fact that we tended to dress up even more. I say "even more" because we lived in an era of dressing up. The idea of attending a party in jeans and a sweater would never have occurred to us - quite apart from the fact that in our early youth jeans themselves were virtually unheard-of, except as tough clothing for manual workers. My father wore jeans long before I did, and it is my clear recollection that I was one of the first girls in the village to possess a pair of jeans. I was then at least seventeen years old. But for the socials we would wear velvet and taffeta and lace, with as many petticoats as we could cram underneath to make the skirts stand out. My own two favourite dresses were one of pink taffeta overlaid with grey lace, and a dark purple velvet which had, I recall, an extremely low neckline. This latter was a present from Aunt-Meg-in-America, which was probably the only reason I was permitted to wear it at all, for it was certainly much more daring than most of the dresses being worn in the village at the time. It should be explained, perhaps, that Aunt-Meg-in-America, my mother's sister-in-law, was at that time the head buyer in the dress department of Sears and Roebucks store in Philadelphia: her idea of a Christmas or birthday present for a far-off niece was to have two or three frocks parcelled up and sent over - a privilege for which I was by no means ungrateful, for her taste tended to run on more exotic lines than that of my mother, and my wardrobe and my status within my peer group both benefited enormously from these regular injections of interesting clothes.

Aunt-Meg-in-America was thus described to distinguish her from Aunt-Meg-in-Scotland, another sister-in-law of my mother. "Muv" as I had begun to call her when I grew out of "Mummy" had been born in Kent, but had grown up mainly north of the border, despite which she remained the epitome of Englishness. Both her brothers, however, had married Scottish lassies, both named Margaret and both known as "Meg", so we distinguished them by geographical references.

Aunt-Meg-in-America was a fiery redhead: a dedicated career woman; hard-working, outspoken and generous to a fault. She and my mother corresponded constantly, but I only ever met her once, long after I had grown up. Aunt-Meg-in-Scotland, on the other hand, I knew well, for she was a regular visitor to our house throughout my childhood. She was a lovely, bubbly personality, the perfect foil for my Uncle Harry, who was a quiet, clever, serious man with an air almost of melancholy about him at times. He was an accomplished musician, his favourite instrument being the saxophone, and his two sons, my cousins Ronnie and Freddie, played the trumpet and the sax respectively. Together they formed the nucleus of a dance band, which played at venues all over eastern Scotland, but which regrettably never performed in Cornwall. Had they done so they might have provided some livelier music for the Socials!

The family quite frequently came down from Scotland to visit: when they did life became very crammed in our little house, which had only two bedrooms. The problem of sleeping arrangements was solved by putting all the women in one room and all the men in the other - the exception being my father, who would happily doss down on the sofa in the sitting room. Father apart, I cannot say that any of us slept particularly well on these occasions, which usually occurred around the end of July when the weather was hot and humid.

We loved these summer visits, however. My mother, in particular, was always delighted to see her own people. Although she got on very well with my father's family and with our neighbours, I had the impression that she always felt isolated in Cornwall. She had grown to love the place, and indeed never returned to Scotland, even on holiday, but she seemed to lack that sense of belonging which all of us need but some of us never find. People tended always to be ultra-polite to my mother; she remained for ever the stranger in the midst. Other than my father's family, I can remember only two people who ever addressed her by her Christian name of Dorothy. She was always "Mrs. Giles" and this set her at a distance from the other women around her, who were "Grace" or "May" or "Annie" or "Lizzie" or "Edith". Perhaps she minded less than I supposed: certainly she never grumbled about the situation, but there was always a touch of loneliness, almost a sadness, about her.

But not when the family came down from Scotland. Then all was laughter and delight, and outings here and there, though Uncle Harry, having driven down from Fife in a Morris 8 on pre-motorway roads, usually preferred sitting on Porthleven beach to any other occupation that might be on offer. I think, in fact, that Porthleven beach on a fine day was probably his favourite spot in the world. Ronnie and Freddie were both hits with the local girls: the latter surprised some members by winning the Youth Club Putting Competition one summer. What they did not know (for Freddie was a modest fellow) was that just prior to his trip to Cornwall he had become runner-up to the Junior Golf Champion of Scotland, and had been lionised in the national press.

In Scotland, of course, golf has always been anyone's game: even my mother, a most unsporty type, loved to boast of an occasion when she had holed in one. Few people locally, however, played golf at that time. It was expensive to join a Golf Club, and the equipment was costly. Porthleven was nonetheless a very sporting place, with better facilities than most of the neighbouring towns and villages. This was partly due to an institution known as Gala Week, held every year at the beginning of August, which raised money for the acquisition of sports grounds for Porthleven. Everyone took part in the Gala Weeks, and in fairness, there was something for everyone, even if some of the occasions billed as "grand" would perhaps have been better described as "modest".

Oh! the glories of those early Gala Weeks! The flags and the bunting adorning shop fronts: the huge greenery arch across the square with "Welcome to our Gala" in letters three feet high; the imposing presence of the visiting battleships out in the bay: the bustle and excitement from morning till night and the almost incessant bombardment from the loudspeaker, urging you to locate "Mr. Odd Socks" and win ten shillings: the sound of the band striking up the same tune yet again........

The whole thing began on a Saturday, with an Official Opening of excruciating pomposity in the Public Hall: it was nonetheless attended not only by community-minded adults, but by hordes of children, who would then parade through the village behind the band to the Recreation Ground, where they would be treated to a free tea and sports, and where the Women's Institute would preside over what, it has to be admitted, was an excellent fête. In the evening there would be games and competitions: sheaf pitching, for instance, when Young Farmers from miles around would turn up to show off their skills and their muscles. In those days you could always pick out the Young Farmers from other young men by their manner of dress - usually corduroy trousers, though some of the trendier ones wore flannels with baggy knees - collarless shirts open at the neck, knitted pullovers in Fair-Isle patterns, even on the hottest days and, as often as not, cloth caps. Their shoes too - if they condescended to discard their working boots - were heavily serviceable. The Young Farmers' movement has come a long way since those days: certainly its members are visually indistinguishable now from the rest of the community, but those boys, laugh as we might at their somewhat rustic appearances, were splendid people, and their whole-hearted enjoyment of entertainments which, in the last analysis, were nothing more than an extension of their daily work, was really rather amazing.

A frequent winner on these occasions was a quite handsome young man called Bill Cooke. In my early teens I was quite a fan of his for a year or so. Years later, when I lived in the country, Bill was a neighbour of ours for a quarter of a century, and I had perforce to watch him grow old and die. Needless to say, I remember him now, not as a gaunt old man, but as a good-looking young one, his sleeves rolled up above his elbows as he tossed a sheaf what seemed an impossible height into the setting sun.

Round about sunset, the Tug o' war (Farmers versus Fishermen) would be held, and at this point Uncle Walter would come into his own. Uncle Walter (my "honorary" uncle, described in "Seagull Morning") was an avid fan of Tug o' war, and loved to act as team coach, casting a near-professional eye over the opposition and shouting "Heave" to his own side whenever he spotted a weakness. The rest of us, meanwhile, would dance up and down, shrieking uninhibited encouragement to our own particular favourites, with many "Oohs" and "Aahs" as the marker flags oscillated to and from the winning point. It was all the kind of good, clean fun which tends more and more to have mockery and scorn poured upon it nowadays, but which was and is a healthy and delightful way to spend a summer evening.

Gala Week would continue on the Sunday with the only form of entertainment deemed appropriate in those days of much stricter Sunday observance - a Carolare. This event, which has happily been revived from time to time in recent years, was an enormous success, and many thousands of people would pack into the area round the harbour to sing hymns and watch the illuminations. Traffic was brought to a standstill from about eight o'clock till the singing was over at around nine thirty, whereupon throngs of people would mill about in the warm summer darkness, reluctant to go home.   I remember one year when our local MP attended the

Official Programme

AND GUIDE

PORTHLEVEN GALA WEEK

2nd to 9th AUGUST, 1947

OPENING CEREMONY SATURDAY, AUG. 2nd

AT 2.30 P.M.

BY HIS WORSHIP THE MAYOR

(Councillor J. H. Adams)

PRICE " " SIXPENCE

PRINTED BY P. S. BREWER, HELSTON

Official Gala Week programme, 1947

Grand Carnival

The Carnival will assemble at 7-15 p.m. in a Yard kindly lent by Messrs. Harvey & Co , where Judging will take place by independent Judges

Prizes will be awarded for the following classes —

Class	CHILDREN	Class	ADULTS
1.	Horse and Rider	1.	Horse and Rider
2.	Pony or Donkey & Rider	2.	Tradesman's Turnout
3.	Decorated Cycle	3.	Historical
4.	Children's Fancy Dress	4.	Trade Advertisement
5.	Comical [Historical	5.	Original
6.	Original	6.	Mounted Trades
7.	Children under 6 yrs.	7.	Other than Trades
8.	Trade Advert. [anything	8.	Doubles
9.	Walking Tableau	9.	Walking Tableau
10.	Doubles	10.	Comical

Entrance Fee—Adults 1/-   Children 6d.

Admission to Yard to see Judging 6d. (no smoking allowed in yard)

A hearty invitation is extended to all visitors and residents to enter the Carnival, who should give their names to the Carnival Secretary by mid-day on day of Carnival.

Route of Carnival—Fore Street, Thomas Street, Shruberry Corner, and back same route to the Square ; then to Breage-side and back to the Yard for presentation of prizes by Mrs. H. Selby

Please show your appreciation of the Carnival by giving generously.

GRAND   CARNIVAL   DANCE

In the Public Hall, 8-30 p.m. to 12 mid-night

Waltz Competition.   Spot Prizes.

(Prizes presented by Carnival Queen)

Music by the " Modernaires " Dance Band.   Ices will be on sale

Admission 3/-

Schedule for the 1947 Carnival

"Jan of Windmill Land" – 1946 (Ref. Ch. 1). Back row – The author, Paddy Rogers, Brian Dunn, Henry Toy, Brinley Richards, Raymond Lyne, Jimmy Harradon, Elizabeth Pascoe, Front row – Olive Thomas, Shirley Pope, Dorothy Richards, Marina Pascoe, Anna Davies

Picking blackberries by
Loe Pool (Ref. Ch. 1)

Father and a friend at
Falmouth Docks (Ref. Ch. 2)

"Doing the filing" – Rogers and Son. (Ref. Ch. 3) Pat Williams,
Angela Macdonald, Winifred Treleven

Some of the staff, Rogers and Son (Ref. Ch. 3). Ronnie Rosewarne,
Phyllis Lanyon, Jack Pryor, Rosemary Gilbert, Raymond (Boy Ray)
Gilbert, Christine English

A Porthleven Procession (Ref, Ch. 4). The small boy carrying
the Union flag is Michael Williams, the author's first godson.
Other walkers include (l. to r.) Rosemary Stephens, Pat
Sandercock, Frank Phillips (with flagpole), Malcolm Eddy,
Mabel Williams, the author, Marjorie Kitchen

Eating cherries with Mabel at St. Peterstide (Ref. Ch. 4).

High jinks at the Choir Social (Ref. Ch. 4).

The Youth Club Dinner. (Ref. Ch. 4). The minister at the head of the table wearing a paper hat is the slightly eccentric and much loved Tom Darlington who spent a number of years in Porthleven. Others present (l. to r. outside the tables) include Roger Lees, Carol Andrews, Christine Giles (the author's cousin), Nora Bawden, Kenneth Bawden, Roy Kitchen, the author, Tom Blewett, Mrs Lees, the Reverend Lees, Mr. Roy Pascoe, Mrs. Mildred Pascoe. (inside the tables, l. to r.) Spencer Richards, Alan Williams, Elaine Evans, Jean Swartz, Opal Rosewarne, Phyllis Arthur, Rosemary Williams, Lorraine Jewell and one girl whose name the author cannot remember.

David Richards.
"Breaking them with a
rod of iron" (Ref. Ch. 4).

Porthleven Girls' Choir. (Ref. Ch. 4). Mrs. Richards is on the left of
the picture. The lady on the right is Mrs. Winifred Hall, the
accompanist, who was also the chapel organist for many years. The
rest of the choir are (back row, l. to r.) Carna Bassett, Lorna Russell,
June Williams, Lorna Barber, Cynthia Pascoe, Heather Williams,
Brenda Williams, Christine Orchard. (Middle row, l. to r.) Estelle
Miners, Evelyn Williams, Anne Symons, Enid Beare, Elizabeth
Collier, Florence Uren, Beth Jewell. (Front row, l. to r.) Shirley
Miners, Jeanette Williams, Rosemary Symons, Jacqueline Eustace,
Brenda James.

"Cousins" Cash Drapers (Ref. Ch. 6). Note the car coming down
Wendron Street: this was before the one-way system around Helston.

The Reverend John Kitchen.
(Ref. Ch. 8). His daring
escape down the Yangtse
from the Chinese
Communists went largely
unrecognised in his native
Porthleven.

Shagwithna and Oithona with their people (Ref. Ch. 8).

Jane (Ref. Ch. 8).

The Reverend Lees "opens" the new Manse curtains (Ref. Ch. 8).

"Those tartan trews!" (Ref. Ch. 9).

A Youth Club discussion group. (Ref. Ch. 9).   The author is
sitting next to Marjorie Kitchen.   The one boy in the group is
Godfrey Richards.

The author with some of the members of her first
(rowdy) Sunday School Class, taken on an
extremely wet St. Peterstide. (Ref. Ch. 9). Bernard
Trudgeon, Peter Phillips, Hugh Trezise.

"The girls were marginally more controllable" A later Sunday
School Class. (Ref. Ch. 9). Rosemary Stephens, Angela
Pascoe, Sandra Jewell, Maureen Bawden, Irene Bawden.

"The Barber's Shop" – Porthleven Carnival. (Ref. Ch. 4). Ronnie Benney is "shaving" Stanley Downing. Looking on (l. to r.) are Keith Benney, André Gilbert and Edward Hendy

Beth – a lifelong friend (Ref. Ch. 3).

Carolare. Greville Howard was a sophisticated man - related, I was given to understand, to the Howards, Dukes of Norfolk and Earls Marshall of England. I happened to be standing near him whilst the singing was going on. At the end of the evening, we sang "When I survey the Wondrous Cross" and a great, glowing cross appeared against the night sky above Breageside. Our MP stood there with tears running unashamedly down his cheeks - a sight I never forgot.

Sunday over, we would revert to the usual junketings - on Monday, August Bank Holiday, there was a gymkhana in one of Ronnie Benney's fields. The Nicholls twins from Penryn usually won most of the prizes in the children's classes, rivalling each other to see who would take home the most rosettes. Jimmy Snell and Durning Richards, amongst others, would demonstrate their skills in the Hunter Trials, scaring the daylights out of the more timid souls if they happened to be standing too close to a hedge when one of them came sailing over. Then it was on to the Carnival: some of the horses and riders would compete in that, also. One annual favourite was a little girl called Estelle Johns, mounted in fancy dress on a fat moorland pony and led by her father. Ronnie Benney, cavorting in drag on his mettlesome hunter, was less popular in that spectators always feared they would be kicked, though no-one, to my recollection, ever was. The Youth Club would usually enter a float. There was one year when our comic entry was awarded first prize, which was promptly taken away from us because one member squirted a water pistol over one of the lady judges, giving her a drenching. For our sins we were relegated to second prize and had to be content with it.

Gala Week would continue its triumphal way with yet more fêtes and concerts. One of these latter, the "Celebrity Concert" was a protracted and sometimes even tedious affair, at which so many encores were given to the visiting artistes that the programme practically doubled in length. Effusive speeches of thanks were then made at the end, and even the most enthusiastic fans of operatic sopranos and international pianists would begin to long to sing "God Save the King" (or in later years "the Queen") and go home. These concerts were, nevertheless, events of considerable quality, and the boredom we sometimes endured could not be laid at the door of the performers, but was usually the direct fault of whoever happened to be compèring the event with more enthusiasm than skill.

I tended mostly to avoid the Celebrity Concerts, which were expensive in any case, and spend my money at the fair which assembled itself round the harbour. This was the same little family-run fair which visited us regularly at St. Peterstide, Porthleven's other great occasion, earlier in the summer. It was not much of a fair by the standards of the bigger ones which came on Flora Day and Harvest Fair to Helston, but there were roundabouts and swingboats and a very fine fairground organ, which was highly popular and could attract considerable crowds. There was also a shooting gallery; all the guns had their sights filed down and were out-of-true, but my father, a trained marksman, had taught me to overcome this small problem, and I managed to win quite a few glass vases and other useless pieces of ornament, some of which I have to this day. In this I could be said to have followed in the footsteps of my Uncle Edgar, one of two of my father's brothers who had drowned on the "Titanic". In his youth, Uncle Edgar was for ever winning prizes for shooting at fairgrounds, and I still have in my possession a matching set of three jugs which he won at the fair the year before setting out, at the age of nineteen, on his ill-fated journey to America.

Traffic to and from the USA was opening up again after the war; most summers saw someone's long-lost uncle or aunt turning up, with cousins who had never been met before. One or two elderly homesick emigrants returned to stay for good; others, probably finding that the Porthleven to which they had returned was by no means the Porthleven they had left, departed again to the land of their adoption. There was one group of them in particular, who lived in the environs of Camden, New Jersey, who used to meet in one another's houses and reminisce about their youth in Porthleven as I now reminisce about mine, and declare that "they were good old days".

They were, indeed, good days, in those Gala Week summers. On the final Saturday, we would parade around the village after dark with torches, a custom which happily still survives. I believe even now the candle grease is something of a hazard, though it is many years since I carried a torch.

Summer ended, we would look forward to the activities of autumn and winter, which were multitudinous. But first there was the annual Music Festival in the Public Hall. In my early teens I used to compete in the elocution classes - I never dared enter the singing. Michael, my erstwhile Flora Day partner, was a fine boy soprano, and regularly gained about ninety marks for the test piece every year until his voice broke. Then his younger brother, John, succeeded him. Do they still sing? It is another of life's great unanswered questions.

There were regular competitors in the Festival - people who came every year - tenors who warbled "Silent Worship" with varying degrees of skill and basses who vied with one another to sing lower and lower notes. Amongst these latter was David Richards, a contemporary and friend of mine whose voice matured very early. He became in adulthood a very fine singer, famous throughout the county, but in those days he was probably anxious to prove that at sixteen or so he could compete with the best of them, and tended in consequence to choose difficult and demanding pieces of music to perform, often from oratorios like the Elijah. There was one occasion when David was due to sing at evening service in our chapel, and my friend Rosa, who was singularly unmusical in any event, and disliked oratorio, sighed, and made the immortal remark "I see David is going to "break us with a rod of iron" again this evening!"

We had some extremely famous people who came to adjudicate the Music Festivals. One I particularly remember was Leon Goosens, the internationally renowned oboist; he expressed himself delighted, both with the standards of performance and with Porthleven, which I am given to understand he subsequently revisited.

The chapels, not to be outdone, would invite famous people to preach. The great Dr. Sangster preached in our chapel on one occasion: we were packed in like sardines to hear him and I cannot remember a word he said, though I do recall that the atmosphere was electrifying and the singing had to be heard to be believed. Likewise, the galaxy of famous politicians who came to Peverell Road chapel to speak at their annual Guild Rallies are chiefly memorable to me, not for the content of their no-doubt excellent speeches, but for the uncomfortable conditions in which we had to sit and listen to them. The MP Ernest Brown, Lord Alexander, and George Thomas (later Speaker of the House and Viscount Tonypandy) all graced that pulpit and on every occasion the building was packed to capacity, hot and claustrophobic. The adults in the congregation probably did not mind this in the least: those of us who still hovered between childhood and maturity only noticed the discomfort and the inordinate length of the proceedings. Why were we there at all? Today, at the same age, we probably should not have been, but we belonged to a generation who did not believe in missing anything, and we lived at a time when young people were far less detached from the world of their elders, and furthermore were not specifically catered for in the way they are today. This may or may not have been a good thing, but it certainly exposed us to all sorts and kinds of influence to which otherwise we might not have been subjected.

There was a considerable choice of activities in which you could join on most evenings of the week. Youth Club was on Tuesdays. We did not have, in those days, so much as a table tennis table by way of equipment: all our activities centred round visiting speakers, (Mr. Frank Strike, for instance, with slides of local wrecks), the Socials and Getting-up-Concerts! This latter I loved. I had enjoyed being in concerts and plays from my very early childhood, doing my first public performance at the age of approximately four years. I loved it. I was hooked! I adored an audience and was a noted player to the gallery. As I grew up, nothing pleased me more than to spend winter evenings rehearsing some play or concert. The quality of some of the plays we performed was, looking back, rather dubious. Maybe I was vaguely aware of this at the time, for I made no show of reluctance when David Richards (he of the bass voice) suggested that I should write a script for a "grown-up" Nativity Play, which the young people of the village would produce themselves and perform for charity in the Public Hall, backed by a choir. The play was duly written, and the Public Hall was filled to capacity to watch it. I still have the press cutting of the time, headed "Teenager writes play", of which I was probably a little over-proud. I also still have, safely tucked away at the bottom of a drawer somewhere, the script, at which I have not dared to look for years, for fear of being horrified by its deficiencies.

That this production went well was due in no small part to the efforts of Mrs. Dora Richards, David's mother. A highly skilled and dedicated musician, this remarkable lady had a girls' choir who enjoyed a high reputation throughout Cornwall and who sang in halls and chapels in all the surrounding villages. Mrs. Richards co-ordinated the choir for the Nativity Play, and also for the Passion Play which followed. For this latter we were even more ambitious; the work involved an orchestra as well as a large cast and a choir. "Teenager writes Crucifixion Play" joined my growing collection of press clippings.

At about this time I joined a choir myself: it was the Ladies' Choir at Peverell Road, with whom I practised regularly every Thursday evening. Our conductor was a Mr. Ernie Bawden, another dedicated musician, who was also bandmaster of Porthleven Town Band. Ernie was a delightful character. He had a highly individual style of conducting - "energetic" is probably the most suitable word to describe it. He would sway and rock and bend from the waist and throw his whole self into what he was doing, such was his enjoyment of the music he was making.

The Ladies' Choir gave numerous concerts around the district - sometimes two in one week at busy seasons like Harvest Festival, when the traditional Monday Fruit Selling was usually preceded by a concert of some sort. Then at Christmas we would combine forces with the Porthleven Male Voice Choir under their conductor, Mr. Ted Wimbleton, to give a joint concert in the Public Hall. This was another packed-house occasion, but for us it was more comfortable, because we were on the stage rather than squashed into what was, at the time, a too-small auditorium.

Mr. Wimbleton was a very different type of conductor from Ernie Bawden. A butcher by trade, he was neat and precise in all his movements, and though I have no doubt at all that he derived tremendous pleasure from his music, he was a great deal more restrained in his expression of it. He was without question yet another of the number of skilled and dedicated musicians who did so much to add culture to the life of our village in that post-war era.

The Public Hall was the venue, not just for concerts and parties, but for more serious events, or at least those which ought to have been more serious. Into this category came political meetings.

I was highly interested in politics in my youth, if a trifle blinkered in my approach. My father was what might have been unkindly described as "a rabid Socialist" - he and my Uncle Norman, his brother, who was a dedicated Conservative, used to have heated arguments on political subjects every time they met. They would get more and more excited; shout louder and louder at each other until their wives despaired of peace ever reigning again. Then, at the end of the evening, it would be "Well, boy, see 'ee again" and they would slap each other's shoulders and part the best of friends.

Unfortunately, Father was not content to keep his political opinions within the confines of the family, and he encouraged me to attend political meetings in the Public Hall with him when elections were due to take place. Neither did he discourage me from sitting with a crowd of young Labour supporters who would barrack the Tory and Liberal candidates and cheer for the Labour. The candidate I remember best in that capacity was Peter Shore. Needless to say he did not get elected for the St. Ives constituency, but we thought he was absolutely wonderful, and of course, once he obtained a seat in the House he went on to high office. Father, meanwhile, would formulate cunning questions with which to entrap the unfortunate candidates fielded by the other parties: the cheers which went up from his cronies when he got to his feet would rival those heard when the Leader of the Opposition stands up in Prime Minister's Question Time. My mother, meanwhile, cringing with embarrassment at all this, would remain firmly at home.

I have voted, in my adult lifetime, for each of the major political parties and for none. I am the floating voter whom every politician needs to woo. But I can honestly say that politics was never such fun as in those heady post-war days when we joined what was then called "the Labour League of Youth" and went round the village pushing leaflets through doors, and held noisy and unskilled debates with our Conservative-minded friends, who were, for the time being at least, our enemies.

Rosa was never my enemy, but she had a cooler head than I and was a great deal less passionate about politics. It was fashionable, at the time, to have an autograph book and get your friends to write in it. Rosa put into mine a quotation from Kipling, which reads:-

"The wisest thing, we suppose, that a man may do for his land

Is the work that lies under his nose, with the tools that lie under his hand".

Meanwhile my own work, as I gained skill and experience, was to become more and still more interesting and was to be the focus of my life for a good many years.

CHAPTER 5

Cases and Characters

I cannot remember the first time I ever went to work in a Court of Law nor, for that matter, the last such occasion. There were many of them, and it was a part of my work in which I took great delight. Perhaps it appealed to my sense of the dramatic: I had always loved the Court scenes in films and plays, and to be involved in such a setting in real life seemed to me a most exciting experience.

The structure of the Criminal Court system has altered so much since those early days of my forensic career that by way of reminder it may be worth explaining how it worked then. The lowest Court, then as now, was the Magistrates' Court for the area, known as the Petty Sessions. The areas covered by each set of Magistrates was much smaller and more localised than it is now, and there were no stipendiary Magistrates - at least not in West Kerrier, the area with which I was to become intimately familiar. Another oddity, by today's standards, was that there was no Court office as such; instead, each Court employed some local solicitor as its paid Clerk: his firm organised and ran all the business of that Court and was, obviously, precluded from involvement in any case which came before it. The two areas I knew best were Helston Borough, of which Mr. J. Antron Thomas of Randle Thomas and Thomas was clerk, and West Kerrier, served by our own Mr. Rogers. We therefore dealt, in the office, with all the Court correspondence, the preparation of summonses and, monthly, the Court agenda. This last was a horrible task: it had to be typed in columns on a huge stencil set landscape-wise in the typewriter. Unfortunately the typewriter carriage was never quite wide enough to allow for the handle of the stencil's backing sheet; this had to be folded under the stencil itself, which caused an uneven surface, resulting in creases and letters which did not cut properly through the wax. Somehow or other, we managed to produce the document, but it was everyone's un-favourite task, and we all tried to be terribly busy with something else when the agenda came down for typing.

The particulars of the cases to be heard included, naturally, the name and address of each defendant, the nature of the charge and the penalty. All this information had, of course, to be precisely correct, and woe betide the typist who got it wrong. There was one famous incident where our senior typist, no less, a lady famed for her accuracy and high standards, accidentally transposed two letters of the simple word "dogs", resulting in the defendant being charged with "keeping two gods without a licence". This gaffe, needless to say, did not fail to attract the attention of the Press, and considerable public hilarity resulted.

West Kerrier, being a rural area, was of course full of dogs, many of them legally kept without licences. The rules were that a pet dog must be licensed (price seven shillings and sixpence per annum) but a farmer might keep up to two dogs without a licence, provided they were employed in driving sheep or cattle. It was necessary for farmers to fill out each year an application form for Exemption from Dog Licence. These forms were obtainable from our office and had to be returned there when completed. They were then stuck on a spike in Reception to await attention. At a particular sitting of the Court they were dealt with, in bulk, from a list which it fell to the lot of the junior typist to prepare. This might seem a simple-enough operation until it is pointed out that the vast number of forms on the spike had to be sorted, first into parishes and then into strict alphabetical order. Oddly enough, I never minded "doing the dog list" which occasionally even provided some light amusement, such as the farmer who wrote "Rover" in the space marked "Name". A true dog lover, obviously.

My real joy, however, was to go to Court, either with shorthand notebook or, on some occasions, with typewriter. This latter was necessitated by a procedure known as "taking depositions" - long since defunct in the Court system and probably not mourned, since it was fairly taxing on those involved in it. Its origins lay in the far past, when the Circuit Judges made very infrequent visits to County Towns, and the memories of witnesses might easily fade before a case came to trial. "Depositions" was designed as a way round this particular problem. Each witness to the case would be called to the stand, sworn in and questioned as to his or her evidence. The questions, with their answers, were transposed into statement form on the typewriter - for example:-

Question: "Where were you on the night of the fourteenth April?"

Answer: " In bed with my wife" would come out in the typed statement as "On the night of the fourteenth April I was in bed with my wife".

When these masterpieces of literature were complete, they were read aloud to the witness who, (provided he agreed the statement) would sign it. This committed him to presenting exactly that same evidence when the case later came to trial at Quarter Sessions or Assizes, and if he deviated from it, someone in those Courts would want to know the reason why. Accuracy was therefore all-important, as was the ability to type at high speed whilst being glowered at by the defendant in the dock, not to mention the patronising gaze of learned Counsel for the prosecution, and the anxious glances of the Clerk. Add to this the fact that four or five carbon copies were needed of each deposition, and you had a fairly tricky job of work on your hands. It was necessary to keep a very cool head in these circumstances: I found that this end was best served by pretending to be a character in a play, which in a way you were, since the well of the Court was always full of members of the public, all agog to know what was going on. Another qualification for success in taking depositions was the ability to spell. In those days there were no spell-checking facilities on typewriters - indeed, the machine I used in my early forays into Court was yet another ancient Remington, probably of pre-war vintage, carried up to the Guildhall from our office for the day. Mr. Rogers challenged my spelling only once in the time I worked in Court with him. The word in question was "broccoli" and he actually adjourned the hearing for a dictionary to be brought, since he was determined to prove me wrong. I was, however, found to be correct and the two defendants, both illiterates who signed their statements with a cross because they could not write their own names were, I hope, impressed. Incidentally, they had been charged with stealing the said broccoli, so it was imperative that the word be spelled correctly!

Some cases were as trivial as the stealing of broccoli, or keeping dogs without a licence, although these latter would not have required depositions to be taken, being dealt with by the Magistrates on the spot, with a fine usually not exceeding ten shillings. I did, however, work on some cases which were very serious indeed, including two famous murder charges, both of which have been described in other books, notably by Dr. Hocking, the County Pathologist, a very familiar figure to me at one time. My own observations on these cases, however, may be of some interest.

The first of the two was what came to be known as the "Porkellis poisoning" and the defendant was a Miss Hargreaves, who lived just outside Porkellis village with another woman, Miss Boston, on a smallholding. I remember Miss Hargreaves as being totally unfeminine, more like a man than a woman in appearance. In Court she dressed in men's clothing, and her hair was cut in a short back-and-sides style.

She was, in fact, an educated and quite cultured person, and perhaps had not deserved the burden fate had laid upon her in the shape of one Albert Massey, the widower of the woman who had been her childhood nanny. Miss Hargreaves had, it seemed, a kindly streak in her nature, and when nanny had died she had promised that she would look after the old widower. He, by all accounts, had proved to be a dirty and disgusting old man, whose habits in the house both she and Miss Boston found unbearable. She asked him to leave and find other accommodation, but he excused himself on the grounds that he was unable to find anywhere suitable. She tried to have him removed but discovered that, legally, she could not do so. It came to her attention, however, that if Mr. Massey left her home of his own accord - say, to go into hospital - she would then be entitled to refuse to have him back, and he would be put into care in an Old People's Home. She decided, therefore, to force the issue by making him sick, and her preferred method was to put weedkiller (Sodium Chlorate) into his food. Unfortunately for her, she grossly over-estimated both the lethal dose and the cumulative effect of this particular poison in the human body. She administered several doses to the old man over several days. He died a horrible death and she was brought to Court charged with his murder. I remember the day well: it had snowed quite heavily during the night and the buses were not running in the morning, so I had to put on my boots and walk to Helston to work carrying with me the black dress and shoes I usually wore in Court. There was a long delay whilst the Police car bringing the defendant down from Exeter got stuck in a drift on Bodmin Moor, and the taking of depositions went on well into the evening, causing me to be late for a fancy-dress party! Fortunately the snow had melted during the day and I was able to return home by bus.

Miss Hargreaves' Counsel was, at her subsequent trial, able to convince the Court that manslaughter, rather than murder, would be the more appropriate charge, and of this she was convicted.

There is an interesting, if hardly amusing postscript to this sorry story. Some time later, her sentence served - I have no doubt she obtained full remission for good conduct - I saw Miss Hargreaves in Helston again. She was in Boots the Chemists, buying Sodium Chlorate in the garden department. Happily, however, there were no further violent deaths in Porkellis; no doubt the driveway at the Hargreaves/Boston establishment was meticulously clean and weed-free.

The other murder trial in which I was involved was one which became famous nationwide, since the two culprits were the last pair to be hanged for murder in this country. I refer, of course, to the notorious "Constantine murder" of 1963. Many accounts have been written of this crime and the subsequent trial, most notably that in "Bodies and Crimes" by Dr. F.D.M. Hocking, who was

County Pathologist at the time. My own highly personal recollections, however may again be of some interest.

Strangely enough, the murder victim had been a childhood friend of my father. They had attended Porthleven Church of England School together, both of them being expelled simultaneously at the age of thirteen for their involvement in a classroom fracas in which the teacher was assaulted. In later life my father was not proud of this episode, and I only mention it to clarify his association with William Rowe, with whom he had kept in touch for a few years after leaving school.

It is, I believe, well-known that Mr. Rowe deserted from the Army during World War One, and disappeared from public view for many years. It was generally supposed that he had escaped to Australia; at least this was what my father was given to believe when he enquired of Mr. Rowe's brothers about his well-being.

My friend Sylvia had lived during most of her childhood on the farm adjoining that of the Rowe family. She spoke of "strange things" there. For instance, on the way home from school she and her sisters would pass an unploughed field; on the way back in the morning it would have been ploughed - this during the long winter darkness. No doubt people had their suspicions, but no-one actually voiced them.

The Rowe family had moved to Nanjarrow Farm at Constantine a few years before the murder. They were clients of Rogers and Son, and Mr. Stanley Rowe, younger brother of the murder victim, would often call in at the office on a Monday when he came to Helston to market. There is a rather strange story about him also. I happened to be in Reception one Monday when he came in as usual and asked to see someone about making his will. "I'm going to die", he declared. Jack Pryor, who was also in Reception at the time, replied jokingly, "So are we all Mr. Rowe". "No", Stanley insisted, "I'm going to die tonight". On enquiry being made as to why he should think such a thing, it transpired that he was due to go into hospital for a routine operation for the removal of his appendix. We all laughed. He made his will, went into hospital, and died that night.

To return to the murder at Constantine, this has been described in plenty of gory detail elsewhere. I was engaged to take depositions for several days in Court at Penryn. Constantine was in East Kerrier, and I was "lent out" for the occasion because I was thought to be the best person to do this particular job. It was certainly not a very easy one. I still remember my sense of shock when I was shown (at my own request) the photographs of the deceased man, lying in a pool of his own blood with his skull battered in. I am glad, with hindsight, that the pictures were black and white, rather than coloured.

William Rowe had emerged from hiding some time before, safe from prosecution on account of the Coronation amnesty given to deserters in 1953. The sad thing is that he would probably not have been prosecuted had he come out years earlier than that. His long incarceration in the family loft, coming out only at night for work and exercise on the farm, had rendered him reclusive: he was unable to meet or easily communicate with people, though he had come into the office a couple of times following the death of his brother. I had viewed him then as a sort of curiosity, and taken great delight in describing him to my father. I could not have dreamed of the horror of my next "sight" of this strange, sad man, who had come to such a terrible end.

Our firm were not clerks to East Kerrier, and were therefore free to be instructed to act in cases before that Court. I was therefore involved, back at the office, in the preparation of Dennis Whitty's defence, if defence it could be called, since the evidence against him was so damning. A Truro firm acted for Russell Pascoe, the other defendant. So I was, temporarily, both a Court official and secretary to the solicitor representing one of the defendants - a somewhat confusing situation.

The case against Pascoe and Whitty was totally conclusive. the only question - and it remains to this day an interesting one - was "Which one struck the fatal blow?" Pascoe, in his evidence, declared that Whitty "Went mad with the knife". Whitty was equally adamant that Pascoe, armed with an iron bar, had bludgeoned the old man to death whilst he, Whitty, had burst into tears. Dr. Hocking's own evidence, delivered at his usual rattling good pace and requiring more than normal dexterity on the part of the Court typist, was that the injuries from either source would have been sufficient to kill Mr. Rowe.

The three young women with whom the two defendants had had a rather peculiar "ménage a cinq" in a caravan near Truro, were all called to give evidence, chiefly to the effect that they recognised the murder weapons and had seen them taken out on the night in question. One of these three ladies, who rejoiced in the name of Esha Sweeney, was a particularly aggressive and unco-operative witness. I was told later that whilst serving a term in Borstal she had led a rooftop protest. I could well believe it. She lounged into the box, snarled out all her evidence through clenched teeth, to the extent that I had to ask the Clerk of the Court to request her to speak more clearly, and generally sneered her way through her examination. I felt that here was someone who was not greatly concerned that murder had been done, and realised that I had been living in very sheltered circles by comparison with these girls, probably younger than I was, who had led such sordid lives and become involved, albeit peripherally, in such a ghastly crime.

I have often wondered, over the years, what became of Esha Sweeney. I should like to suppose that she became a reformed character, settled down and raised a decent family, but I fear that is an unlikely supposition, the odds of life being stacked against her.

Pascoe and Whitty sat, side by side in the dock throughout the several days of deposition-taking. Neither of them looked at, or spoke to the other throughout the entire proceedings. It was inevitable that they should be found guilty when the case went to trial at Bodmin at the Michaelmas Assizes. It was also inevitable that they should hang for their crimes. I remember the day of the executions - appropriately a cold, bleak one. Although I was in a better position than most people to be fully aware of their guilt, I still felt a painful compassion towards them that morning. I had long believed (in the academic sense) in the tenet that "murder by the State is no less murder than murder by the individual" and oddly, I believed that most strongly when I had been confronted in a deeply personal way with the horror of what these two young men had done. They had killed for gain and had gained nothing. They had spilled the blood of a harmless old man who had already suffered out of all proportion for his own "crime" of desertion. My father, himself a decorated war hero; holder of the Croix de Guerre, was quite devastated. For my part, I nonetheless felt spiritual and mental pain on the day when they hanged Whitty and Pascoe, and was glad when shortly afterwards the bill to abolish capital punishment passed through Parliament. Oddly enough, I am less sure now, having lived long enough to see the effects of that Act. But it is the nature of the elderly to become uncertain about things - and of the young to know they are right. I was young then, and I was one hundred percent certain that Capital punishment had been rightly abolished.

The sheer futility of the murder itself is best illustrated by describing its aftermath, in which I was not involved. Mr. Rowe had left no formal will, but he had left instructions as to where his not inconsiderable fortune could be found. These instructions were written in Esperanto, which he had taught himself during his years of self-imposed incarceration. When deciphered, they revealed a sum of well over eight thousand pounds - quite a lot of money in those days - hidden in various caches around the farm, including under the floor of the pigsty. Pascoe and Whitty could never have found them, if they had stayed to search the whole farm for a month.

Not all the Court cases I attended were grisly murders. Some, I have to admit, were extremely dull - fraud in particular, where there were always masses of documentary evidence to be sifted through, and numerous experts called to comment upon it. Others were vaguely amusing - like the paternity case where the alleged putative father, having sworn that he had "never gone to X......... in a taxi" was then confronted by the driver who had taken him there and, not one whit abashed, compounded his own perjury by declaring, insouciantly "**H**'all right, **H**'I'll say **H**'I did   go to X.............. in a taxi..." Presumably he felt that the addition of the superfluous aitches added style to his tangled evidence. The Court found against him, and he was ordered to pay maintenance, which he very rarely did, and was often hauled back to account for his arrears. His excuse was usually the stock one offered by small debtors - that he had been off work sick "with a bad back, your Honour" - a bad back being the most difficult of conditions to disprove. Invariably a new job had been lined up to be started the following Monday: and as night follows day, the back was again "bad" by the time Monday arrived.

The strange thing was that we grew almost fond of our little band of feckless, inadequate people and were reluctant to exert upon them the pressures which were legally available. So they would wander from Court to Court, making the same excuses in each and being greeted by the same shrugged shoulders of those whose duty it was to attempt to deal with them.

I have always been aware that I was, to some of my friends, an object of pity because I had not gone to college; not obtained a degree and, in their opinion, had no proper career. "A boring little job in a solicitor's office" was how they would sum up my admittedly meagre attainments. Yet by virtue of my exposure to the sharp end of life, having to encounter hardened criminals and assist, albeit at a rather basic level, in the administration of justice, I am sure that my job was far more exciting than the "careers" of some of my critics, who plodded sheep-like into the fold of the teaching profession, which no doubt had its own excitements, but nothing to compare with the majesty and the mayhem of the Law! My regret, if I have one, is that I did not avail myself of the offer of articles extended by my employers and become a full-blown member of the legal profession. There were several reasons for my rejection of this golden opportunity; perhaps the true one is that I was enjoying life so much at that time that I felt no inclination to return to what would have been several years of arduous study.

Office life itself was enjoyable, though we all affected to find it a chore. But our days were filled with amusing incidents and colourful characters, many of them the type of person not easily found nowadays. One such was a Mr. Ernie Jenkin from Brill, Constantine. Ernie was one of the last men I can remember who dressed for Market Day in breeches and leggings. He topped these with an ancient black jacket, beginning to go green with age, and a bowler hat. He talked with a lisp, largely because he had lost several teeth, and presumably could not be bothered to obtain a set of dentures. He liked nothing better than to encounter his old rival-in-love, Mr. W.B. Peters of Mainlay, Cury, and engage in a verbal sparring match. One of these two gentlemen, I cannot remember which, because their stories varied so much, had filched the girlfriend of the other one Flora Day (or was it Harvest Fair?) some forty or fifty years previously. It was hilarious to hear these two old men still contending for the charms of a lady neither of them had married and who was, it seems, long dead by then anyway.

Another farmer who frequently called in on a Monday was Mr. A, whom I shall not identify. This gentleman, unlike Mr. Jenkin or Mr. Peters, did not dandify himself to come to market. Indeed, he would come in wearing the same clothes he had worn to milk the cows and muck out the sties. Consequently there was an odour about him which was somewhat less than pleasant. I well remember one very wet winter Monday, when it was bitterly cold, this gentleman had been in to consult Mr. Rogers, whose next appointment was with two very prim spinster ladies, retired teachers both, coming in to sign their wills. I needed some information from Mr. Rogers, and ventured into his room between appointments. His window was wide open, as it would have been on a summer day. A howling gale was blowing papers off the desk. The following conversation ensued:-

Me: "Sir, why have you got your window open like that?

Mr. Rogers: It's because I've had Mr. A. in here, and the Miss So and So's are due next - I'm afraid they'll think it's me, smelling like that."

Happily, the Miss So and So's were just a little late: the window was able to be closed, and cups of tea were served in the approved manner and in the normal, rarefied atmosphere of the senior partner's room.

Occasionally, I was required to take notes at inquests - these could be particularly harrowing occasions, both because of the high speed at which you had to write, and also because of the content. Dr. Hocking was always much in evidence on these occasions, and he would rattle off complicated medical terms at a great pace, making me glad that (a) I could write very reliable shorthand and (b) I had learned Latin at school - it helped tremendously from time to time.

There was always an element of sadness at inquests, especially when bereaved relatives were present, hearing the details of how their loved ones had died, either accidentally or deliberately. One of the worst occasions was the inquest into the infamous Darlwyne tragedy, when the pleasure boat of that name had sunk off Dodman point with the loss of a great number of lives. The Court room that day seemed to be full of learned Counsel, each representing one or more of the bereaved families, and it was quite difficult to sort out who was representing whom, and what needed to be recorded and what did not. Transcribing the notes took several days and I was quite exhausted at the end of it.

Possibly the saddest inquest of all, however, was that held after the deaths of a retired judge and his wife, who lived at Ruan Minor. This couple had married late in life; she had formerly been his housekeeper. They had died together in a fire at their home. The pathological evidence that day made very painful listening indeed, and one could only hope that the deceased persons had lost consciousness rapidly, before they were fully able to realise what was happening.

The deaths of the Judge and his wife raised complicated legal problems. He had been relatively well off: she had very little money. He had left his fortune to her or, if she predeceased him, to a couple of his favourite charities, there being no children of the marriage. However, the law says that where a couple die in circumstances such as theirs, and it is impossible to say which one died first, then the younger is presumed to have survived. The lady was younger than her husband, so the presumption was made in her favour. This meant that the nominated charities would get nothing, even though the husband's intention had clearly been that he would provide for his wife during her life and that the charities would benefit after her death. The situation as it stood meant that her relatives, none of them particularly close, would inherit all his fortune. Happily, they decided to do the honourable thing: the charities received lump sum payments from the estate and everyone was at least partially satisfied.

Wills, of course, make fascinating reading, especially old ones. I remember in my very early days at Rogers and Son being given one to read in which the testator had left his barn doors as a specific legacy to one of his nephews, and a set of chamber pots to another. Since both these beneficiaries had had considerable expectations of their uncle, they must have had quite a shock when the will was read.

"Reading the will" after the funeral is something which is rarely done nowadays, if indeed it is done at all. But when I first started work it was not an infrequent occurrence, and sometimes led to quite a fracas. I remember an occasion when one of our clerks returned from the funeral of a highly respected local farmer who had quite a large family of equally respected grown-up children. Our clerk described in detail how punches had been thrown; women had pulled one another's hair; insults had been traded and hysterics indulged in, to the extent that he had had great difficulty in finishing the reading of the document.

If wills were troublesome, however, their absence was even more so. On the other hand, this presented wonderful opportunities to explore other people's homes, and I have had some delightful times going through drawers and cupboards in the houses of deceased people in search of the elusive document. Most memorable among these occasions was when I was summoned to

Tenderah, an enormous house opposite the Grammar School, which was then the home of the Misses Tyacke - or more properly, of Miss Tyacke, since one of the ladies had recently died. She was known to have made a will, but it could not be found, and her sister, who was elderly and in poor health, was adamant that she would not "have a man rooting about the place". So the task fell to me. I was conducted by the surviving Miss Tyacke into a room of faded splendour which had once been a dining room but had clearly not been used in that capacity for many years. There were two large tables in the room, each measuring something like 5 ft by 9 ft or even 10 ft. Each of these tables was literally a foot or eighteen inches deep in loose papers - old letters, inside and outside of their envelopes, postcards, family photographs, bills, receipts - none of them attached to the invoices to which they related - water-colour paintings, finished and unfinished, bits of blotting paper and old Christmas and birthday cards going back almost to the turn of the century. "I am sure", said Miss Tyacke, "That the will is somewhere in here". Initially my heart sank, but I gradually warmed both to my task and to my hostess, who sat in a chair with her bad leg up on a stool, and regaled me with tales of family life in the Edwardian era when her parents were alive and she and her brother and sisters were young. Her father had been Mr. J. Walker Tyacke, a well-known Helston solicitor and predecessor of my own employers. I had already heard many stories about him.

One, concerning his detestation of the telephone, always struck me as particularly funny. He had grudgingly allowed JPR, then a young solicitor in his employ, to have the phone installed in the office. Its number, which was unchanged when I first went there to work, was Helston 9, so we are talking about the very early days of the telephone. JPR, amongst his other tasks, was at that time acting as solicitor to the Penrose Estate.

His cousin, Captain Lionel Rogers telephoned with a query on some legal point, and the phone rang in J. Walker Tyacke's office. "Is Mr. Rogers there?" ventured Mr. Lionel in reply to the barked "Hello!" "I don't know" retorted Tyacke "You'd better come up and look". He then put the phone down. So much for technology and progress.

Miss Tyacke, as I searched for her sister's will, was able to tell me other fascinating family stories, including how she had personally gone to India to bring home her niece and nephew after one of her sisters had died in that far-off land. It was obvious to me that she was a sad, lonely lady now, living with her memories of better days.

I found the will, about halfway down the pile on table number one, and was almost sorry to have done so, for I was enjoying myself immensely. Even the clutter on the table was intriguing. A stamp collector, for instance, could have had a field day there. I never called on Miss Tyacke again - to do so would have seemed vaguely improper - an intrusion into a way of life which no longer existed. She did not live long after that, but I shall not forget her, nor the fine, faded house which was Tenderah at that time.

Our managing clerk had a much less romantic experience searching through the effects of two old brothers who had lived near Constantine. They had kept their money in the approved fashion, under the mattress, and it had to be got out. Unfortunately, by the time they had died, the mattress had become very soiled and verminous, and the task was more than a little nauseating. On his return home, Jack immediately got into the bath where, he told us, he counted no less than forty two fleas floating on the water, brought home in his clothing.

By contrast, the home of the late Miss Magor, where I went to assist Dougie Charles with an inventory, was a habitation of cleanly perfection. Miss Magor, it appeared, had inherited the house from the previous owner, whose servant she had been. She had continued to maintain the premises to a very high standard: to this day I can still almost smell the beeswax and lavender which pervaded the air in the quiet, elegant Georgian dwelling at the bottom of Coinagehall Street. The antique furniture glowed: the linen was starched and crisp: the dainty china ornaments were in pristine condition and the brass and silver gleamed. Shafts of sunlight fell on polished floors which seemed to me almost too beautiful to walk on. The whole thing was reminiscent of the stage set for a refined period play.   I never knew Miss Magor, but I remember her house with great delight. She had obviously cared greatly about it: I hope it gave her as much joy as the memory of it gives me.

Very gradually, like dry leaves quietly falling on a still autumn afternoon, many of the old clients of the firm, like many of the old characters of the village, were passing away. The word "deceased" appeared on the covers of files of people who had until recently been regular callers at the office: you missed them - missed the quaint, anachronistic traits which made them stand out in a world in which they really no longer fitted and with the ways of which they found it impossible to conform. They belonged to that lost time of horse-drawn carriages, bowler hats, stuffy front parlours with horsehair sofas and oil lamps lit in the evenings. They were strong people: they had survived two World Wars. They had seen the railway arrive in Helston: likewise the motor car and the aeroplane. They had come to terms with the existence of things like radio and the telephone, and the more flexible spirits among them were capable of being enthusiastic and fascinated by the post-war era with its constant stream of change and discovery. But it was, for all that, not the world they loved best, and many of them, I am sure, were not entirely sorry to leave it. By contrast, we who were young then thought our world a marvellous place. Harold Macmillan told us we had never had it so good; perhaps politically this was a simplistic statement, but increasingly, with the war years behind us, goods more plentiful in the shops, no great shortage of jobs and a reasonable sufficiency of leisure, we found a great deal in life in which to take delight.

CHAPTER 6

A Time of Transition

AT no time in history had this area changed so dramatically as it did in the years between 1945 and 1955. Much of this transformation emanated directly from Culdrose, and the impact it had upon the neighbourhood. In "Seagull Morning" I have tried to describe the infinite sadness of seeing well-known farms disappear under the airfield: as time went on we became used to that idea, but it was fascinating - at some levels horrifyingly so - to witness the astonishingly rapid development of what is now the largest helicopter station in Europe, with the consequent urbanisation of what had previously been a tranquil rural area, albeit somewhat lacking in material prosperity. The whole ambience of Helston, for instance, inevitably changed for ever, though happily some of its best old traditions managed to survive and indeed to prosper. Flora Day, for instance, still attracts huge crowds, and perhaps they are larger because of the involvement of the Navy in the occasion.

The children of naval personnel naturally attended local schools. At first their arrival was a thin trickle, which only later became a flood. Certainly in my time at Helston Grammar you could identify the handful of "Naval Children" quite easily. They tended to arrive in mid-term and had to be slotted into the appropriate year, often finding some difficulty in adjusting to a different curriculum from the one they had been used to in Portsmouth, or Lossiemouth or wherever it was they had come from. Some of them stand out in my memory, notably one Dick Cardwell, a jolly little chap who arrived in the first form during my final year. Dick was the eldest of four Cardwell children, who all attended Helston Grammar, the family having settled locally.

There was at that time a thriving and profitable pig farm in operation at Culdrose. Dick and his brother Chris both took weekend and holiday jobs there, helping to muck out, and it was thus that they met my father, who was at that time in overall charge of animal management. Father grew very fond of the two Cardwell boys, though he was for ever lecturing them on safety matters - not without cause, as it turned out, when an unwise brush with a boar in father's absence resulted in Dick sustaining a badly lacerated leg. He adopted a more cautious approach after that - at least so far as the porcine population was concerned - he was ever a bold spirit in most respects.

Another "Naval child" whom I particularly remember was a girl named Erica Wheeler - a thin, pale, blonde little soul, beautifully spoken and rather sensitive. Like me, she wrote poetry, and I was extremely taken up with a piece entitled "The First Chrysanthemum" which she published in the school magazine. I should have liked to have been friends with Erica, but cannot say I really succeeded. There was always a slight distance between her and the rest of us which was difficult to bridge. She was indefinably but certainly "different". Maybe nowadays this sort of problem no longer exists - I hope it does not - but the dilemma of adjusting to new people from an alien background was still quite real in those days, both for us and for them. One would have supposed that coping with the evacuees during the war would have solved the problem, but I was very much aware that some of these successors to the evacuee population found their new environment quite intimidating and some of their Cornish schoolfellows perhaps just a little less welcoming, at first, than they might have been. Happily, the young always adjust very rapidly to change, and before long the "Culdrose children" were no longer considered remarkable in any way, and hopefully found themselves by-and-large well-received both in school and in local society.

It was not just schoolchildren, however, who were affected by the coming of HMS Seahawk. The sudden plethora of young men in the area had an obvious effect upon the adolescent and young adult population. Girls, in particular, found themselves spoiled for choice of partners at dances; the result of this novelty was that local boys, unused to serious competition, sometimes found themselves rather left out of things. It may not have been a direct consequence of this, but it is certainly true that at that time there grew up a fashion amongst local boys for a Saturday night exodus "down West" where many of them found themselves girlfriends - and subsequently, wives - from Marazion, Penzance and Mousehole.

Some of the stricter local parents deplored the possibility of their daughters marrying into the Navy, and some went so far as to forbid them to go out with sailors at all. Given the protective climate of the times toward young women, this is perhaps a little more understandable than it would be today, but one suspects that the real fear of these parents (apart from the obvious one) was that their beloved daughters would be whisked away to live in Scotland or Hampshire and their children, in turn, would not be properly Cornish, would not grow up locally, would not go to school in Helston and might never dance the Flora in their entire lives! These fears, however, were always cloaked in a good thick layer of moral disapproval in relation to which "She goes out with sailors" became, in some circles, a term of aspersion almost comparable to "she is a loose woman" - a regrettable manifestation of the worst kind of xenophobia.

Like all garrison towns, however, Helston came to terms with its own destiny. Porthleven, likewise, saw many happy and successful marriages between local girls and sailors from Culdrose, a pattern which continues to the present day, when with the increased mobility of society the mountain of yesteryear is not even perceived as a small molehill.

It was during the mountain years, however, that Ted turned up at our chapel. Ted, who was to become a lifelong friend of mine, was a young Petty Officer, then recently drafted to Culdrose, who had previously been based at Lee-on-Solent. There he had made friends with someone whose mother happened to live in Porthleven. When it was learned that Ted was coming to Culdrose, he was given Mrs. Mitchell's address and the rest is history, at least in the annals of the chapel. Ted came down to tea one Sunday and was taken to chapel in the customary way. He was fond of singing (he had an excellent tenor voice) and joined the choir. From then on he was integrated into the church community and after some vicissitudes eventually became - and remains - a Methodist Local Preacher. But before then he was joined by others from Culdrose, their names and characters indelibly written in the memory. There was Arthur Miller, a garrulous and entertaining Irishman; John Peacock - quietly spoken and usually rather serious, but having a strange habit of suddenly breaking into comic recitations; Trevor Locke, pint-sized and rather timid - an orphan who had been brought up at naval boarding school with no alternative choice of career on offer; and Bob Jarrett who, being a steward with sea-going experience, was extremely useful on social occasions because he could rush about carrying a tray with two layers of cups and saucers on it and never spill a drop! These boys and others whose names I have forgotten were like a breath of fresh air in our rather close little community, and helped, probably without knowing it, to widen our horizons and, in the words of the hymn "enlarge our scanty vision". What happened to them? John Peacock, on leaving the Navy, became a Vicar in the Church of England: Trevor Locke, against all the odds, went to work as a missionary in the Church of South India. Bob Jarrett married a local girl, lives in Tiverton and still visits Porthleven frequently. Ted himself, after a post-naval career in HM Customs at Dover, now lives in Bude with his wife, Eve, and habitually comes to Porthleven where, in some sense, part of him will always belong, like a thread woven into the complicated tapestry of our village history. Perhaps he was less the thread than the needle which pulled it, for he unwittingly spearheaded a process by which naval personnel ceased to be regarded as curiosities amongst us, but were accepted - or rejected - for themselves, rather than the uniform they wore.

Interesting as the impact of Culdrose was on the life of the community, it was the economic expansion it effected which perhaps had the greatest significance. To begin with, it created - and continues to create - jobs - much needed in a community whose young male population were newly returned from war. Large numbers of men and women found employment "on the camp" and this in itself did much to break down the early barriers of hostility and suspicion. The building trade flourished as Naval housing estates were erected on the outskirts of Helston. One of the last of these to be built became the cause of a considerable war of words between the Vicars of Helston and Breage. The latter, who rather prided himself on his aesthetic taste, launched a broadside in the local paper, complaining that the houses there were "little boxes made of ticky tacky" and a visual disaster. The Vicar of Helston, who saw himself as a reformer and attached enormous importance to social issues, retaliated the following week to the effect that these were "homes for people" and as such should not be denigrated. The name stuck, however. To this day one hears occasional references to people living "Up the Ticky Tacky". Meanwhile the local shops - particularly in the early days when out-of-town supermarkets were not even a dream of the future - did rather well out of the growth in the population. Inevitably, Helston itself changed. Indeed, for a few years the commercial heart of the old market town became rather like a game of musical chairs. Mr. Jackett-Simpson, for instance, moved his garage from Coinagehall Street to Meneage Street. There was one enormous public benefit deriving from this: the new premises actually had a forecourt: you no longer had to step across the hose which led from the petrol pumps on the inside of the pavement when a car was being filled up in the street, as you had to do at the old premises. They were taken over by the Post Office, who modernised them extensively. Their old premises at the bottom of Meneage Street became a fruit shop, and remained so for many years.

Next door, however, Cousins Cash Drapers continued as it had always done - a beacon of stability in a changing world. This amazing and wonderful emporium stocked all manner of ladies' clothes, haberdashery and linens, and in the main enjoyed a reputation for modest prices. The most remarkable thing about the establishment, however, was the air of extreme informality with which the staff tended to treat not only each other, but the customers who came into the shop.

A rather hilarious incident comes to mind which illustrates this. I had been invited to a summer wedding or some such occasion, and needed a new hat. Not being particularly well-off at the time, and knowing that Cousins had a fairly good range of reasonably priced headgear, I made my way there one Saturday morning before going in to work. I was in consequence rather early; in fact, I was the first customer in the shop. Several pairs of eyes scrutinised me as I walked in. No-one moved. No-one spoke. No-one smiled. A little unnerved, I approached the owner of the nearest pair of eyes with a hopeful expression on my face. "Yes" she snapped. "I'd like to see some hats, please" I ventured. Ignoring me completely, she hailed the senior assistant, a Miss Anthony, addressing her thus "Miss Ant'ny! 'Ats!" Miss Anthony obligingly came forward and led me down to the basement, where she clicked on the lights, directed me to where I might find what I was looking for, and disappeared back upstairs, leaving me to my own devices. It has to be said that I had a high old time, trying on at least half the stock, including models much more expensive than I could afford. Time went on. I looked at my watch and I looked up the stairs. No sign of Miss Ant'ny. I had been given half an hour off work to come and buy my hat, and time was running out. Finally, not without some reluctance to leave this Aladdin's cave of millinery delight, I picked up the black straw creation I had selected and took it back upstairs to the ground floor. Miss Ant'ny was leaning, arms akimbo, on the polished wooden counter, chatting to one of her minions. A look of sheer amazement crossed her face as I appeared. "Aw!" she exclaimed "You! I forgot all about you." It was, as they say, par for the course.

Miss Ant'ny was one of two sisters, short, rather stout identical twins, who were well known Helston characters. Unless you knew them particularly well, you could not have told them apart. Keen churchgoers, they represented "old" Helston - the town as it had been before Culdrose; before the war; before anything that had happened to make things different. At the core of any Cornish town you would find such people, and they were the heart of the place. They lived where they had always lived; in many cases in the same houses where they had been born, and in which they had grown up. They understood local traditions and participated in them with gusto for as long as they were able. They spent the winter anticipating the delights of Flora Day or, in the case of Porthleven, St. Peterstide. Imagining ourselves, at seventeen or so, much more modern and sophisticated, we tended rather to treat this sort of person as a joke, and to view ourselves as enlightened and progressive. Strangely, those of us who remain in the area have now come to cherish the old town traditions in much the same way as our forbears did, and are no doubt the object of the same benign condescension on the part of the young. Will the same metamorphosis happen to them? Will they, too, learn to cherish old and simple things? Will the old ways survive? Perhaps, with determination, the best of them will, and those which do not were maybe not worth the preservation.

The other great factor of change in those years of my early youth was, of course, the advent of television. This did not arrive in the remoter regions of Cornwall until several years after the end of the war, due largely to problems with reception, which remained extremely uncertain for quite some time. "Snowstorms" frequently obliterated favourite programmes, usually at their climactic points, thus completely spoiling the entertainment for new and dedicated viewers. In spite of this, many people persisted in acquiring sets as soon as any signal could be received at all, and when you went into their houses would triumphantly switch on the test card to show you what splendid reception they had.

I cannot say that I was greatly drawn to television in its early days; most of the programmes appeared puerile and down-market. There was, however, the famous occasion when Dylan Thomas' "Under Milk Wood" was being shown on screen for the first time. I had seen a production of this play in London and was determined to watch it. Grace-next-door was for ever urging us to come round and watch TV at her house; my father, keen on sport, had done so once or twice in order to watch football, but I had not availed myself of the opportunity. However, I plucked up courage to ask Grace if I might watch her set on that particular evening and with her usual generosity, she agreed without demur. I turned up at the appointed time and the set was already on. Reception was grey and rather blurry, but the sound - which after all is the important thing in "Under Milk Wood" - was clear enough and I settled down for what I hoped would be an enjoyable hour or so. Unfortunately, neither Grace-next-door nor her best friend May, who was also present, was the type of person to appreciate the rich language and characterisation of Thomas' play. They quickly and obviously became extremely bored; this made me feel exceedingly uncomfortable and I did not quite know what to do. May solved the problem by keeping up a constant barrage of conversation. She was making nets at the time - an accomplishment at which she was deft and at which she spent most of what passed for her leisure. "I'm 'ere strugglin' wi' these ol' nets" she confided " 'An Graace is relaxin..!'" More conversation followed in the same vein. In the end, had it not been for the fact that the Cornish accent is entirely different from the Welsh, one would have been hard-put-to-it to know whether May was in the room or whether (which seemed more likely) she was actually a character in the play, who had somehow contrived to walk out of the screen.

I thanked Grace prettily for her kindness in letting me watch the set, and secretly resolved that if I ever again wished to view anything which might classed as mildly "highbrow" I would seek a venue where the company shared my own taste. This became increasingly easy; more and more people acquired television sets, and the inevitable result was that local organisations and events were much less well supported. People "could not come" because their favourite programme was on TV. Furthermore, the fact that the on-screen productions were wholly more slick and sophisticated than the amateur efforts of local people on stage in the Public Hall gave people a standard of comparison they had previously not had. Not unnaturally, people were growing reluctant to pay two shillings (or two-and-sixpence, in some cases) to watch what was, quite frankly, inferior entertainment.

Over the years, however, this has resulted in huge efforts being made towards excellence. No-one nowadays would dream of trying to get away with the kind of crude, unaccomplished and sometimes downright bungled productions which at one time formed a focal point in village life. Not only did people look for better; they began to understand that they themselves were capable of better. This was the positive reaction to television; the negative one was that you had to work twice as hard as previously to arouse public interest in any event you were trying to put on. Time has gradually reduced the impact of this phenomenon, but in its infancy television inevitably became, for a while, a severe problem to those who tried to foster community life outside the home.

Alongside television came, of course, the growth of motoring. People who had never owned cars in their lives began to acquire them and to go on longer and longer excursions. Trips to Plymouth, for instance, at one time a once-a-year affair for most people, became quite commonplace, although until the opening of the Tamar Bridge in 1961, getting into Plymouth on a Saturday when Argyle were playing at home could be a long-drawn-out experience, as the queue for the Torpoint Ferry reached mammoth proportions. The ferry itself was not always entirely reliable. On one famous occasion my mother and I had gone to Plymouth on the coach, and on the way home the ferry broke down in the middle of the river. It was a beastly cold, wet, rough November night, and we wondered whether we should have to spend it in its entirety stuck halfway across the Tamar. Eventually, with much grinding and groaning, the hapless vessel was got going and we finally creaked to shore in Torpoint, arriving home more than two hours late. It was a long time before I could persuade my mother to go to Plymouth again.

My father did not favour coach trips, preferring to borrow a car for special outings. He was a highly accomplished driver - indeed during his sojourn in the United States in the 1920s, he had on one occasion chauffeured the Vice President, something of which he was intensely proud. Usually, if we were having a family outing, he would borrow a taxi from his brother, my Uncle Dick, for whom he often worked at weekends. On the particular occasion I have in mind, however, all the taxis must have been booked, and we were going to visit another uncle, Norman, in hospital at Tehidy. There lived in Porthleven at that time a very generous man named Bill Eddy, who owned a small and ancient car which was affectionately dubbed "The Violet" after Bill's father's fishing boat of that name. Bill was always willing to lend The Violet to any competent driver for the purposes of hospital visiting, and so it was that we set out in that vehicle one summer Saturday evening to visit Uncle

Norman. Saturday evenings, then as now, tended to bring out droves of young men who saw themselves as fine drivers and wanted to show off their imagined skills by speeding along the roads. The Violet was not really up to speeding, and we chugged along comfortably enough, being overtaken by car after car after car. It was as we passed through Trewennack that a large Ford shot past us, honking his horn in derision at The Violet's slow and stately progress. Father's patience snapped. He, who had driven the Vice President of the United States in a multi-cylinder Cadillac, was being honked at by a mere youngster in a mere Ford! Angrily he leaned out of the window, shaking his fist at the disappearing overtaker. "That's all right my son" he shouted in his fine broad Cornish accent, "This car'll be on the roads when yours is on the scrap heap". I cannot of course comment on the outcome of this prophecy; suffice it to say that The Violet sailed on and on and on, although Bill eventually gave in and bought a newer model, if only to get to work in Camborne more easily.

It was not just cars which were gathering pace; life itself was doing so. Those of us who were still very young did not really notice at the time, but the whole ambience of Porthleven and the surrounding area was changing. Old men still sat on the seat at the foot of Salt-Cellar Hill, as they do to this day - but passers-by were beginning to be less liable to stop and chat to them. Women increasingly were going out to work, and had less inclination to hang about gossiping in shops. Tea meetings - once a feature of autumn afternoons in the chapels - gradually ceased to be, as fewer and fewer people remained available to attend them. School leavers were going away to university in ever-increasing numbers and many of them were opting for careers which kept them out of Cornwall for the rest of their lives - or at least until their retirements. Thus, whilst more and more people moved into the area, more and more of the indigenous population moved out. In many ways, this was probably a healthy thing. Doctor Elliston had always said that Porthleveners were "interbred, underfed, and a damned lot of lunatics". Perhaps he was in a particularly choleric mood when making that somewhat exaggerated statement, but there was a grain of truth in it. The village in which I had grown up was extremely introverted. The village in which I spent my teenage and young adult years was becoming ever less so, and for better or worse the new and the different were here to stay

CHAPTER 7

"The King is Dead"

ONE of the most important aspects of growing up is the dawning recognition of the fact that life is a very impermanent business: that the safe structures of a happy childhood are eroded by many changes and in particular by the demise of loved and valued people. In my own life, it was probably the deaths of my father's brothers, always thought of collectively as "the uncles", which served as a series of sharp reminders of the more painful aspects of human living, and the need to develop the resilience to cope with the inevitable blows which fall from time to time.

My uncle Henry died when I was thirteen: it was the first death in our family since that of my paternal grandmother when I was just three. I can remember my grandmother and I can remember the day of her funeral and how I spent it, but I cannot say that the two were in any way connected in my mind at the time. Grandma had been ill and I had not seen her for a while. The funeral took place from our house, but I was not present. I was taken to lunch with friends - we had baked egg custard for pudding - and afterwards went for a long walk in the lanes outside the village. On my return home, the house was full of aunts and uncles, all of whom made a fuss of me and kissed me - some of the latter with bristly moustaches which scratched my infant skin. Gradually they left and it was bedtime: the usual routine of a story and prayers. A week or so later I was taken to the cemetery to "put flowers on Grandma's grave" and I do not remember even remarking the fact that Grandma had died. It was an event I took entirely for granted, though I had been very fond of the old lady, who was a sweet person and very gentle with children.

By contrast, ten years later, I was both saddened and fascinated when Uncle Henry died. He was the third eldest of my father's eight brothers, and was some fifteen years older than my father. For most of his life he had worked as a gardener, an occupation at which he excelled, and latterly he had been in charge of the gardens at Belmont, just outside Devoran, which belonged to the Simmonds Hodge family. I had spent many happy hours at Belmont during my childhood, playing in the stable yard in the sunshine or, on wet days, burying my head in one of Cousin Isabel's large collection of "Just William" books.

Uncle Henry "took after his mother" both in appearance and in personality. Whereas many of his brothers (my own father included) tended to be somewhat fiery, even quarrelsome characters, Uncle Henry was by contrast quiet and comforting; I had always found him an easy person to love. His final illness, swift but painful, took place in the cold spring of 1947. I have a vivid and detailed recollection of what I was doing when the news of his imminent death reached me - I suppose in much the same way as people effect to remember precisely what they were doing when President Kennedy died. We were, I recall, in the throes of rehearsing for an end-of-term play at school, and I had consequently stayed late that particular afternoon for a dress rehearsal. Whilst awaiting my turn to go on stage, I was parading about the school hall in a long blue evening dress belonging to the games mistress; various boys from our form were prancing about in brightly coloured doublets and hose and the atmosphere, as is often the case on such occasions, was quite hilarious. Suddenly the headmaster came in, grave-faced, with a message from my parents, who had gone that day to Devoran to visit Uncle Henry. He was terminally ill. They would be late home and I was to go to Aunt Edith's house after school, and wait for them there.

It was a strange, numb feeling. Dear Uncle Henry, warm and jolly and delightful, would soon be gone. I suppose this was the first time I ever became properly aware of death, and of its effects upon people.

The aftermath of Uncle Henry's death was particularly sad for his immediate family. My aunt was compelled to move, at very short notice, out of the little house at Belmont, with its lovely, old-fashioned cottage garden, its rambler roses and its lilac bushes. It was a tied cottage and the owner wanted it immediately to house my uncle's replacement. My mother and another aunt called on Aunt Minnie very shortly after the funeral and found her in the throes of packing - she was deeply distressed; still in shock from the death of her husband, and my mother, normally the mildest of women, was extremely angry at the callous way her sister-in-law was being turned out of her home at a time of great housing shortage, with no time given to look about for somewhere else to go. My father and his brothers raged at the injustice of the system, but there was nothing they could do. Isabel and her husband, who had just moved into a house in Devoran village, took my aunt to live with them, and she spent the rest of her life there. For my part, I was inculcated with a lifelong horror of homelessness, which has never left me and I suppose now never will.

We were never a family much given to visiting one another's houses - we had only gone to Devoran two or three times a year and these outings, given the vagaries of the bus service, especially during the war, were in the nature of major expeditions, with queues of up to an hour for each of the three separate buses which had to be caught en route. Nevertheless, the death of Uncle Henry changed things - you felt there was a hole in the backdrop of your life and I was well aware - for the first and obviously not the last time - that things would never be quite the same again.

I was seventeen before the next death in the family - that of my Uncle Jim, my father's eldest surviving brother. He, being twenty years older than my father, had always tended to fill for me the role of a grandfather, both mine having died long before I was born. Certainly he had always been extremely indulgent to me in my childhood, showering me with gifts of fruit when I visited him at Penrose Gardens, where he worked, and taking me for rides in the hackney carriage he drove in his spare time for his friend John Williams (known as John the Gardener). John's hackney ponies were a well-known sight around the village, and frequently competed in shows throughout Cornwall.

The passing of Uncle Jim deprived Porthleven of one of its larger-than-life personalities. Jim Giles was his own man; strong of character and something of an eccentric. Even his style of dress was singular. I well remember him going out for the evening, smartly attired in old-fashioned breeches and leggings, the latter highly polished, with a bowler hat tilted slightly forward on his head, and a small carnation in the buttonhole of his black jacket. This whilst riding an elderly and extremely upright bicycle down Peverell Terrace!

124

Uncle Jim frequented a certain public house in Helston, where he was well-known and somewhat feared by some of the other regulars. Amongst these was a rather unpleasant little man whose name, for obvious reasons, I will not state. This person was standing at the bar one evening, slightly inebriated, boasting of his imagined pugilistic exploits. Someone warned him "Jim Giles will have you" to which he retorted, "I'd like to see him try..." The words were barely out of his mouth when he felt a hand at the back of his neck. He was then lifted by his coat collar, carried at arm's length, struggling like a fish on a hook out of the bar into the street, where Jim Giles deposited him in the "kennel" the stream which runs down the main street of Helston.

Besides being a keen gardener and a skilled horseman, Uncle Jim was extremely fond of dogs. In my childhood he had a black Labrador, a boisterous animal which would leap at you as you came through the door and bid fair to knock you off your feet. By contrast, in old age, Jim acquired a very stately Pyrenean Mountain Dog, to which he gave the improbable name of Buster. Buster was the sort of dog who would happily let you into the house, but showed extreme reluctance to allow you to leave. On one occasion my Uncle Dick was visiting his brother and got up to go home, whereupon Buster placed himself in the doorway and growled. Uncle Dick, not unnaturally, hung back. "He's all right, he won't hurt you" Jim assured his brother, whose reply "I've heard you say so: I haven't heard him say so" has gone down in the annals of family history.

Uncle Jim represented, in many ways, a world which no longer existed: it was to his credit that he remained respected in the society he perforce inhabited, but in which he manifestly did not truly belong. It is good to be able to remember such people.

My father's family was to be further decimated over a short space of time. It occurs to me that "decimate" is a highly appropriate word to use, since there were originally ten of them! Uncle Norman died when I was nineteen and my father was deeply affected by his death, since they were next to each other in age. As children they had been extremely close, sharing a bedroom, their secrets and as often as not their well-deserved punishments for various offences, including that of playing truant from school. There was one famous occasion when a ship had been wrecked off the Lizard, and Uncle Norman and my father decided to skip school and walk around the cliffs to see it. They had been instructed by my grandmother to collect five loaves of bread from the baker's on their way to school; this they did, and took the bread to the Lizard with them. Unfortunately, they became extremely hungry and there was no bread left when they arrived home. My grandmother was not pleased at having to turn-to and bake bread that evening and the three boys (my Uncle Edgar was with them) were sent supperless to bed.

The Giles family lived well outside the village, and in consequence the boys often got very wet walking to school in the rain, so much so that they would often be sent home again lest they caught a chill by sitting about in wet clothes. It occurred to them that they could capitalise on this; they devised a system whereby, if it had been raining, and stopped, they would get into a convenient large puddle and douse themselves with water, so as to arrive at school soaking wet. This worked well for a time or two; unfortunately one day, as they happily splashed each other, my grandfather looked over a nearby hedge and saw them. Norman and Ned scampered off to school; refused to be sent home and never tried that particular trick again!

The day of Uncle Norman's funeral is etched indelibly into my conscious memory. He was a popular person and in consequence the event was well-attended and in accordance with the custom of the times, there were a great many floral tributes, one of which, from his grandson Colin, was of yellow chrysanthemums. The weather that day was foul, and as we entered the cemetery there was a sudden huge gust of south-west wind. It blew the petals off one of the chrysanthemums, and to this day I can see them, drifting over the wet grass as we made our way to the graveside, like bright memories of times gone and people who were disappearing all too rapidly from our purview.

My father was destined to live to quite a good age, but soon all but one of his brothers were to be gone. Uncle Dick died when I was twenty. Silver-haired, erect and very smart, he was always regarded as the "gentleman" of the family: indeed I cannot remember seeing him dressed in anything but a well-pressed suit, in strong contrast to my father, whose sartorial preference ran to baggy flannels and dreadful old cardigans! Uncle Dick had started a small taxi business in 1928, with an Austin 18 car. The business flourished, and he added some fine pieces of engineering to his stable, including an Alvis Crested Eagle and my own favourite, an Alvis Silver Eagle, though these were largely laid up during the war years, owing to petrol rationing. There was also a Humber Pullman, out of which I once fell through leaning against the door when it had not yet been properly shut. Fortunately for me, the car was not in motion at the time: on the other hand, Uncle Dick was just arriving outside to close the door before driving off: I fell at his feet and he trod rather heavily on my fingers!

Dick Giles died in high summer, and his funeral was held on an oppressively hot day. My strongest memory of the occasion is of being driven very slowly down Peverell

Terrace with other members of the family in a closed car, with the sun beating on the windows. Uncle Dick, experienced in such matters, having been the driver for many families in similar situations, would no doubt have appreciated our discomfort, and told us to open the windows and let some air into the car. But Uncle Dick was gone, and another small segment in the annals of village history was over.

My father grieved for each of his brothers in turn and for all of them in an ongoing sense. After each bereavement, his boisterousness and his sense of humour would gradually return, but there was a definite though barely perceptible diminishment of both. He was no doubt beginning to feel that sense of impending isolation which all of us experience if we outlive our contemporaries and siblings. For the rest of his life Father was painfully aware of being the survivor - although he had one brother still alive, my Uncle John in Pennsylvania, with whom he began to keep up a much more assiduous correspondence as the family circle on this side of the Atlantic shrank into nothingness. Uncle John was a horse trainer, and continued in that rather glamorous and very exacting occupation until he was well into his eighties, when a kick from a colt put him into hospital, and he decided it was time to retire. In spite of being ten years older, he managed to outlive my father by several years, and died well into his nineties.

The regular succession of deaths in the family inured me to the inevitability of the matter. With each one I found myself increasingly able to cope with the fact and the prospect of bereavement. These, however, were personal deprivations, and remain so. I still miss the Uncles, that big, jolly, amusing cast of people amongst whom I acted out the simple dramas of my childhood and early youth. The death of the King was different. It was and was not a "family thing". It was a matter of state but seemed to affect everyone in a personal way. This was, in retrospect, quite amazing, given the restrained social climate of the age and the general distaste for the kind of emotional exhibitionism which, for worse or better, seems since to have become fashionable.

I was not quite eighteen years old at the beginning of February, 1952 - my birthday would fall later that same month. The news of the royal death was brought to us in the office by, of all people, the caretaker of Barclays Bank next door - a retired army man rejoicing in the name of David Disraeli Dunn, who was known as "Dizzy" Dunn. Dizzy was one of the characters of Helston. An inveterate gossip, he seemed always to know everything about everyone, so that bringing news of the King's death was almost by way of a scoop for him; he had beaten both the radio and the newspapers and made his announcement with an air of solemn triumph. We were dumbfounded; we had known the King to be ill, but it had not occurred to us that he was likely to die, though older people had probably envisaged the possibility. However, the mystique which still tended to surround the Royal Family at that time would have precluded any detailed discussion in the press about the symptoms of the monarch's illness. Dizzy's announcement therefore brought a considerable sense of shock, for the King was a popular man, and not old.

At that time we used to receive a delivery of the Evening Herald at the office just before we left work. That day's issue was bordered in purple, as were most newspapers during those sombre times, when normal radio shows were cancelled and solemn music was played continually over the airwaves. On the day of the funeral local businesses closed for an hour: I went to Helston Parish Church to say a prayer which I could perfectly well have said in the office or in the park, but I felt the need to make the effort, being then as now a convinced royalist. I knew very few people at that time who were otherwise persuaded, and had never met an out and out republican. True, there were those who grumbled at the bill for the Civil List: most people, however, accepted the cost of the monarchy as a part of life and quite sensibly took the point of view that the maintenance of a president and his or her entourage would probably place at least an equally great financial burden on the electorate - perhaps more so, with the cost of a presidential election added every four years. Besides, you could never ensure that the chosen president would be suitable for the office, not having been "bred to it" after the manner of royalty. It must be conceded that this particular aspect of the argument was weak and illogical, given the many monarchs in British history who have themselves proved to be square pegs in an extremely round hole - but our then recently deceased King did not number among them, in spite of the disadvantages under which he had laboured on coming relatively unprepared to the throne. Because of him, we had come to expect quiet dignity and reliability in our head of state, and we had no reason to suppose that this situation would not continue. I cannot, of course, speak for people as a whole, but that was how it was in the (admittedly limited) circles in which I moved; we were almost fiercely royalist; we were saddened that Our King had died, but we believed wholeheartedly in the capacity of the new young queen to continue the work her father had begun; indeed, for those of us who were young ourselves, her youth and undeniable prettiness added glamour and sparkle to the role she must play.

It was therefore with a high sense of anticipation that we approached Coronation year, during which all the usual festivities and junketings were due to take place. Most of these (children's sports, presentation of mugs etc.) duplicated similar efforts in other local towns and villages: others were unique to Porthleven. One such event, memorable for its awfulness, was the embarrassingly bad production of a rather disastrous play written "especially for the occasion" by Mr. George Knight, an elderly retired journalist who lived in Thomas' Street.

It is worth digressing to talk about Mr. Knight, who was a cultured and erudite man and a very interesting personality. A classical Greek scholar, he once kindly gave me a Greek/English Lexicon, a copy of "Teach Yourself Greek" and a Greek New Testament "so you can learn to read the New Testament in its original language". I still have these three books and at one stage endeavoured to make proper use of them, though I cannot say I ever became very proficient in New Testament Greek: nevertheless I remember Mr. Knight with pleasure and gratitude.

In spite of - or maybe indeed because of - the fact that he was so scholarly, George Knight was unfortunately not cut out to be a playwright. The piece he wrote to celebrate the Coronation was entitled "The King of Prussia Cove" - a lengthy, one-act affair based on the doings of the infamous smuggler, John Carter. I remember initially being offended at not being invited to audition for a role in what was being billed as an important production: in the end I was grateful to have been left out of what proved an extremely wooden affair with a highly improbable script. Its presentation was not greatly improved by the fact that very few of the actors seemed to have bothered to learn their lines properly, so that the audience heard nearly as much from the unfortunate prompter as they did from those on stage. Neither did the producer appear to have paid a great deal of attention to stage movement, with resulting chaos as people obstructed each other's passage on and off stage; moved in front of whoever happened to be speaking, trod on one another's feet and generally milled about in almost total confusion, with no-one seeming to know where he or she ought to be at any given point in the proceedings. Mr. Knight himself played the part of the chief Revenue Officer; his portrayal was not entirely convincing, even at the visual level, since he was then over seventy years of age and had a huge thatch of unruly white hair, which made him look more like an Old Testament prophet than a rugged enforcer of the law in 18th Century Cornwall.

Nevertheless, the King of Prussia Cove provided us with a great night in the best old Porthleven traditions; we roared our support for the smugglers; cheered and clapped in all the wrong places; were convulsed with laughter when we should have been serious, and generally entered, if not into the spirit of the play, at least into the time-honoured unruly traditions of the theatrical Pit - something which George Knight himself may well have appreciated, when all was done.

I cannot remember whether the play preceded or followed Coronation Day; certainly the day itself was remarkable for other things. I spent the morning glued to the radio: few if any people in the village had acquired a television set at that time. In the afternoon the rain went off sufficiently to enable the children's sports to take place. In the evening there was probably a dance in the Public Hall: there was almost always a dance in the Public Hall in those days on every special occasion. I did not go to the dance; the Youth Club, of which I was secretary, had a special invitation to attend a firework display at Culdrose. For this event we had hired a coach, and the members turned out in good numbers, highly excited to be included in the Navy's guest list for the night. Unfortunately for us, the driver of the coach had been celebrating rather freely all day and was decidedly the worse for wear by the time he picked us up. Somehow he wove his unsteady way to the main gates of the camp and somehow he wobbled back again, but the whole occasion was spoiled for us by the terrifying journey, clinging as we were to our seats and to each other as our conveyance narrowly missed hedges and went round corners on the wrong side of the road. We were certain that we should have a head-on crash, which I suppose was a strong possibility, especially if our inebriated driver had "met himself" coming the other way, since I do not for one moment imagine that he was the only drunk driver on the roads that night. Hopefully, however, he was the only one in charge of a coachload of vulnerable teenagers!

I should like to suppose that such a situation could never occur nowadays, but one cannot be sure; certainly it was an experience I never wish to repeat and although the firework display was excellent, we could not truthfully say that it crowned the day. Roy, our Youth Club Leader, was furious, and told the proprietor of the coach firm in no uncertain terms that if there was ever any question of that particular driver being in charge of a coach we had hired, he could expect no more business from us. From then on I noticed that the proprietor himself always drove us on all our outings, whether to Gwennap Pit for the Whit Monday service, or to Plymouth for the pantomime in January, or to any other venue.

Any sense of flatness we may have had in the days following the Coronation was well and truly countered by the impact of the Coronation Film, which most of us went to see at least twice. Huge, excited queues formed daily outside any cinema where this feast of ceremonial was showing. The romance of the golden coach; the magnificence of the greys drawing it; the elaborate and intricate detail of the embroidery of the queen's gown; the glitter of gold and jewels under the Abbey lights; the sumptuous robes of the peers; the sheer glory of sound as the trumpeters sounded the fanfare and the choir burst into "Vivat Regina"; one viewing; one hearing, were totally insufficient to take it all in. It was something beyond anyone's recent experience: we had not long emerged from the national debilitation engendered by World War II - and for those of us too young to remember any pre-war splendour, this was something beyond our imaginings. Even my father was sufficiently moved to put aside his socialist leanings and declare "There's no country in the world can put it out of hand like we can". This reference to British expertise with high ceremonial was something with which few people would have dared to disagree. To disapprove was another matter. There were detractors - indeed, there always are those who invariably deprecate grand gestures - even the Bible contains an instance of this. "The money should have been used to feed the poor". If this argument had been applied to the Coronation, two questions would have needed to be answered; "which poor?" and "how many of them?" - since even the cost of this country's great day would have done little to alleviate human suffering on the grand scale. As it was, though the expense fed no starving bodies, it was a feast for hungry spirits. It would be some time yet before Prime Minister Macmillan's most famous and much disputed utterance "You've never had it so good", but that day in June 1953, as the queen went to her crowning, there was a new feeling of confidence in the air. The bad times, it seemed, were now well and truly in the past. We were entering the New Elizabethan Age - and if that was an illusory perception, we could not have been expected to know it then. We felt good. We were young: life was opening up to us; we looked to a bright and beautiful future in this new queen's reign. The king was dead. Long live the Queen!

CHAPTER 8

Context and Contrasts

THE introverted cultural and political attitude of most small towns and villages is a well-known phenomenon to anyone who has ever lived in that kind of setting. It is probably part of the charm of a place; certainly if it must count as a character defect it is one shared by the vast majority of small communities up and down the land. It finds its focus in a concentration upon "local issues" Thus, things vastly important on the international scale fade into pale insignificance beside such weighty matters as the overflowing litter bin on the town square, or the uncut grass on the verge beside the river, or whether or not there is sufficient lighting in the main street.

Porthleven was and is no great exception to this general rule; it is a place where a certain amount of dust is usually being raised about some issue, great or small, affecting its own internal life and the comfort of its inhabitants. To a very large extent, this is a natural and proper thing; we concentrate on putting our own house in order before trying to set the world to rights.

Notwithstanding this, astonishing events occurred on the world stage in those years of my growing-up; events which changed the entire nature of life on this planet - yet they elicited scant attention in my home town, which pursued its egocentric way from local crisis to local crisis and, at least on the surface, shrugged off any undue concern for cosmopolitan affairs, good or bad. Maybe the more thinking individuals, especially those of riper years, gave due consideration to what was going on in the world at large; I have to admit, however, that most members of my own generation were not notably concerned with those things. The causes of this omission were probably multiple. The "careless rapture" of early youth, for instance, was for us conjoined with the fact that we had lived, in our thitherto short lives, through a World War of dramatic proportions and were consequently blinded to the possibilities of anything much worse ever occurring. Again, maybe the fact that world news coverage had not reached the saturation levels of the present day had something to do with our complacency about world issues. At this space of time it is impossible to say. It is nonetheless true that for the most part we went about in relatively blissful ignorance of the more painful aspects of current affairs, even though some of them touched us much more nearly than we were aware.

In 1949, for example, Mao-tse-tung and his communist cohorts took full control of China, an event which had the immediate result of persecution for Christian missionaries in that vast country. Amongst these was a Porthleven man, John Kitchen, referred to briefly in "Seagull Morning" as the weekly beneficiary of prayers from the Sunday School Superintendents, offered on behalf of "Brother Kitchen in far-off China". Brother Kitchen, who was on the staff of a Christian mission in Chengtu, close to the Tibetan border, became an early target of the communists. He had served in China for over thirty years, operating, amongst his other activities, a Christian printing press, which issued publications in four languages. His first wife had died tragically in a plane crash, and he had eventually re-married, his second wife being Norwegian - hence the name of their baby son, Olav. With the help of some Chinese friends, Mrs. Kitchen managed to leave China with Olav strapped to her back: her husband, accused of being "a spy for imperialistic forces" was detained and put under house arrest. He was then given an exit permit, only to have it withdrawn and be put under house arrest again. Eventually, with the aid of a servant and a colleague, he slipped out of the house early one morning and made good his own escape down the Yangtse, disguised as a fisherman (an appropriate form of deception, given his Porthleven roots and fisherman forbears!)

Yet this extraordinary event made scarcely a ripple on the calm surface of Porthleven's life, though this was one of the town's own sons, involved in the kind of audacious adventure about which whole books are written. But it happened to a modest man "in far-off China" and though it was spoken about it was apparently not nearly so newsworthy in the village as, for instance, the complicated negotiations to acquire land for the new football ground!

This protracted affair dragged on for several years: in 1949 over eight hundred local inhabitants signed a petition to the Council to exercise its powers of Compulsory Purchase without delay; but in the event the matter was not settled until 1952, and even then the Order needed some amendments in 1953. The longed-for football ground, however, once acquired, became a jewel in our local crown and remains a vastly important feature of the town today.

Indian Independence came, of course, earlier than this, in August 1947. I was still at school then, but I do not recall any information being imparted or comment made by any member of staff on the subject. They may have supposed that the matter was too weighty for the average thirteen-year-old, and they may well have been right. My father and his brother Norman, however, had a spirited debate on the situation. Father was much in favour of independence and greatly admired Mountbatten for his handling of the hand-over: Uncle Norman was disgusted by the whole affair and declared that we had "lost India". "Damn me!" Father replied, "We've gained India!" His reasoning, not particularly hard to follow, seemed to be that we should be popular in that land for having given them what they wanted. With the advantage of hindsight, it is fairly easy to see that quite of lot of them did not get what they wanted, and the feuding between India and Pakistan, more than fifty years on, bears witness to this.

In Porthleven, at that time, the burning topic of the hour was not who would get which part of the Indian sub-continent, but which families would be allocated the first available new Council houses: those who were fortunate enough to acquire them were in every sense of the word deserving people, but this did not prevent a considerable public furore breaking out amongst others who perceived themselves as equally deserving, but not as lucky.

In 1950 the Korean War began. This conflict has recently been dubbed "The Forgotten War" and not without some justification. Various local young men fought in Korea, and had a hard time there. Amongst them were Mainor Ruberry and Willie Pascoe. Willie was already married at that time: his first baby son, Mark, was born while he was away. A gentle person, with a great concern for the welfare of children, he apparently spent most of what little spare time he had in Korea visiting and helping out in orphanages. Mainor, who quite often used to come down to play soldiers with us in The Gue when we were children, narrowly escaped death on the ill-fated troopship, Empire Windrush. Happily both he and Willie survived to return home, but there were many up and down the land who did not. For their families and friends, their loss was just as real as any incurred during the World Wars, but somehow people in general did not seem to relate to it in quite the same way, and the anxieties of those whose loved ones were serving in the danger zone then were not publicly perceived at the same level as they would have been between 1939 and 1945.

Meanwhile, the Town Clerk of Helston was writing a somewhat prevaricating letter to the Secretary of Porthleven Gala Week, making excuses for the fact that little progress was being made in the matter of the purchase of land for the football ground. The reasons he gave make interesting reading: they included Rate-Making, a Borough Council Election, Flora Day, the District Audit and the Duchess of Kent's visit to Helston. This last I well remember: the Duchess (mother of the present Duke) wore a royal-blue outfit with a white hat and gloves. The Duchess had always enjoyed a reputation for great beauty and it was something of a disappointment to me to see her looking so very "ordinary". I do not know quite what I expected from someone in middle-life on a rather dull, cold spring afternoon in Helston, but I had hoped for just a little more glamour. That she was a charming lady with a warm smile could not be denied, however, and we applauded her arrival generously. Hers was the first royal visit to our area since World War II and she was, therefore, the first member of the Royal Family I had ever seen in the flesh.

A year or so later, on 31st October, 1952, Prince Philip himself arrived in Porthleven in his capacity as Patron of the National Playing Fields Association to inspect progress on the new football ground. There was an embarrassing incident on this occasion, as HRH walked close by a local lady not noted for her reticence. Glaring at the prince, she declared, loudly enough to be heard at least 200 yards away, "I thought 'ee was s'poased to be 'ansum. I do call 'un breb'n ugly". (For the uninitiated, "breb,n" is a local colloquialism for "considerably" or "greatly"). The lady was, of course, entitled to her opinion, but there were those amongst the official welcoming party who could have wished she had kept it more to herself, at least for the time being.

The football ground had finally been acquired, not without all manner of incident, including ongoing "guerrilla warfare" between the Council and Ronnie Benney, who quite properly insisted on his right to continue to grow broccoli on the part of the land acquired from him until such time as the Gala Committee should erect a suitable fence. Ronnie appears to have won this battle and harvested his broccoli; the fence was, of course, erected in due course and life in the village continued much as before. Prince Philip in fact later paid us a second visit on 17th May, 1958, at his own request, to see what further progress was being made with the new facilities, with which he declared himself impressed. There is no record of his being insulted about his appearance on that occasion.

Halfway across the world in this same time-span, the Suez crisis was taking place. Willie Pascoe, who had been demobbed, was called up again as a reserve, though happily he was not sent to the action zone on this occasion. This was a blessing for him and his family, for the Suez affair was a cruel conflict with much loss of life. My own cousin, Ronnie, who was serving with the Marine Commandos, was sent to Suez straight from his preliminary training, and later gave me a horrifically detailed account of their landing there. "We were on the landing craft" Ronnie related "And the sergeant told us to keep close by him and jump off immediately after him when he gave the signal. Then he jumped overboard and was blown to bits in front of us". Ronnie, a phlegmatic enough character, would shudder when he told that story.

There is a happier and much more amusing tale about Ronnie, who was one of my Scottish cousins. When he was stationed in Plymouth, after Suez, he found it most convenient to come and stay with us in Porthleven when he had weekend leave, rather than make the lengthy trip to Fife and back. I invited him to accompany me to chapel one Sunday evening, an invitation he accepted. He did not think, however, that his casual clothes were suitable for chapel, so he changed into his uniform, taking tremendous trouble with polishing his shoes, blancoing his belt etc. We set out for chapel and were greeted at the door by the steward, an elderly and somewhat strait laced gentleman. Ronnie solemnly swept his hat off in the steward's direction, and only then remembered that, in common with many servicemen, he had a pin-up photograph of a very scantily dressed young lady inside that hat. The steward, to his credit, raised his eyebrows but slightly and made no further comment.

On another occasion we were with Ronnie in Plymouth, with another friend, Michael, who hailed from Kent and was stationed at Culdrose. Michael had a girlfriend at home in Kent, Judith, with whom he was much in love, and he always bought small presents for her wherever he went. On this particular day he purchased a bottle of lily-of-the-valley perfume, very sweet, heady and feminine. Unfortunately, someone accidentally barged into him on an escalator and the bottle of perfume broke in his pocket, enveloping him with the odour of lily-of-the-valley, which emanated from his person for the rest of the day and resulted in a great deal of ribbing, both from the irrepressible Ronnie and from our fellow-passengers on the coach home.

Neither Michael nor Ronnie opted to stay on in the services at the conclusion of their National Service. Michael, so far as I am aware, never saw action during his time in the RAF: Ronnie purported to have seen enough to last him a lifetime, a sentiment shared, I imagine, by most people who have taken part in any form of war. Certainly the threat of renewed hostilities was never far away in those years. The Berlin Wall went up; the Berlin airlift took place. Patriots in countries like Czechoslovakia, Romania, Albania, Hungary and Poland "disappeared" into communist-run jails. In Russia itself, intellectuals like Solzenitzyn went to the Gulags; Jews were persecuted and were refused exit visas and ordinary citizens went about in fear of the midnight knock at the door. Other nations, even the great USA, felt threatened, and the gathering of military and political intelligence became an art form. The spy novels of writers such as Graham Greene began to appear in bookshops and libraries, feeding a mounting curiosity about the iniquities of life under Stalin and his successors. It seemed that the "peace" we thought we had arrived at in 1945 was nothing but an illusion. As Janie Laity observed to Uncle Walter one fine autumn afternoon "The Book do say there'll be wars and rumins (sic) of wars". One is reminded of the fact that Janie had a daughter-in-law, Marie, who was Hungarian and who for many years was unable to return home to visit her family in that benighted country.

Janie herself was a character - small of stature but extremely outspoken. She almost always wore a navy-blue "tam" hat and a brown, belted mackintosh, making concession only to the hottest summer weather, and even then the hat usually remained firmly on her head. Janie was known for her sayings, sharply observed if oddly phrased at times. Uncle Walter, being a near neighbour of hers, was the recipient of quite a few of them. There was, for instance, the famous occasion when, toiling up Cliff Road on a hot day, laden with bags of shopping, she encountered Uncle Walter in his front garden. "My dear Walter" she exclaimed "I bin (have been) downlong fer me shoppin! Trouble is, 'ee's (there are) so many ol' 'ills to go up when you do go downlong!

Janie had a total disregard for English Grammar, for the letter "H" and in many cases for pronunciation, though she came out with some delightful verbal substitutes of her own. During a time of shortage, not long after the end of the War, she was in Blight's shop trying to cajole Mr. Needham into selling her some ham, which he explained he did not have. "Aw, Mr. Needham" exclaimed Janie "'aven't 'ee gawt a bit in the figgilator for me?" To this day, I occasionally refer to "the figgilator" instead of "the fridge". It was a good word and deserved recognition.

Janie was one representative of a generation of Porthleven women who coped with hard lives and expected nothing different. She had her opinions, however, and was never slow to express them. During 1953 a new minister arrived at our chapel, the Rev. Lees, who held pacifist views. This was something of which Janie did not and could not approve. She had always associated pacifism with the Christadelphian sect, which had a branch in Porthleven. Complaining to Uncle Walter about Mr. Lees' opinions on the subject, she pronounced "I do 'ear that new minister down chapel is a Christadelphian!"

I came to know Mr. Lees extremely well in the five years during which he lived in Porthleven and served our chapel, and although I did not agree entirely with his point of view, I always respected him for it and I have to say that he could put his case in a compelling manner. As a Christian, he believed he ought not to and could not do anything to injure his fellow human beings, whom he would bend over backwards to help in a practical way. I was a frequent visitor at the Manse when he lived there: he had two sons, Ronald and Roger, both of whom became close friends of mine, and their mother, a lady of great warmth and charm, was the kind of person in whose home her children's friends are always welcome.

Informality was the order of the day. It was the most unmanselike of manses! Roger, a fervent devotee of the motor-bike, had a dreadful old machine which was always breaking down, and which he seemed constantly to be in the midst of repairing. He had a habit of wandering into the sitting room with a carburettor or some such thing in his hand, putting it down on the mantelpiece whilst he drank a cup of coffee, and then wandering absent-mindedly out again, leaving the oily artefact behind to catch the eye of any squeamish chapel dignitary who happened to call. Roger was also an early rock 'n roll enthusiast, in contrast to his elder brother, a promising classical pianist who managed to get himself accepted for the Royal Academy of Music and thus departed out of our lives, at least in term-time, though for a year or so there were still jolly gatherings in the holidays, when Ronald, probably to prove that he was not irretrievably wedded to Chopin or Beethoven, would fool around on the piano and lead the assembly in silly songs such as the "Old Lady who swallowed a fly", and we would all talk and argue far into the night.

The Lees household was also inhabited by two tortoiseshell cats, who rejoiced in the highly improbable names of Oithona and Shagwithna. Neither of them was particularly beautiful as cats go: perhaps their names were chosen to compensate for their somewhat homely looks, though they were nice, friendly little animals. For a time, there was also a dog at the Manse, a Great Dane named Jane. Jane had an uncontrollable desire to get into the middle of whatever was going on; it did not matter

144

whether you were dressed for dog-walking or turned out in your very best Sunday-go-to-meeting clothes; Jane would hurl herself at you with abandoned joy and stand on her hind legs to embrace you. Since in that posture she was liable to be taller than you were yourself, it could be alarming if you were not aware of her utter docility. This latter, however, did not extend to the Manse furniture, which she held in undisguised contempt and attacked with vigour whenever she could.   Sadly, her depredations reached a point where it became necessary for her to move to a home where the at-risk furniture actually belonged to the understanding, dog-loving occupants, rather than to the meticulous, hard-to-please authorities of the Methodist Circuit.

Jane's disdain for the Manse furniture was at some levels quite understandable. Circuits in those days did not see any reason for keeping their ministers in luxurious surroundings, and only the minimum of money was ever spent on that sort of thing. Mildred Lees regarded it as something of a triumph when she obtained permission to acquire new curtains for the dining room - the old ones were in tatters. She was not expected, however, to choose expensive material, nor to have the curtains professionally made: in the end they were run up on my mother's sewing machine, but they certainly improved the appearance of the room.

Whilst we trifled with the small problem of the manse curtains, however, the powers-that-be in the world were confronting the global unease created by the "Iron Curtain". Relationships between the West and the Soviet Union seemed to be deteriorating by the week, and the world was being seized with a great and abiding fear of the atom bomb.   This was perhaps the one major international issue which did strike home to us all, reminding us of the underlying threat to our complacent young existence. I was disturbed enough by the situation to write a poem entitled "Child of Hiroshima" which I recited at a local concert, and was invited to publish in the "West Briton". It was intended as a plea against future atomic warfare; unfortunately a certain well-known stalwart of Helston British Legion, a man I quite respected, totally misunderstood the mood of the piece, and supposed me to be condoning the atrocities committed by the Japanese in world War II. Nothing could have been further from my mind: I was horrified when his retaliatory salvo appeared in the following week's paper and found the whole situation and the attendant adverse publicity quite humiliating. On reflection, this was neither the first nor the last time my literary motives had been misunderstood: one becomes hardened to such things in the long run, but unjustified criticism when you are very young is an off-putting sort of experience. It did not deter me, however, from continuing my anti-atomic stance: I was and am against the use of nuclear power of all descriptions, given its potential for wrecking life on the planet. "Stick to your standing" my father used to say "If you don't sell a ha'porth". I may not have sold a ha'porth, but time has yet to prove me wrong on that particular issue. In the matter of energy resources, as in other world affairs, and indeed in the affairs of Porthleven, there has to be, as St. Paul told the Corinthians "a more excellent way".

CHAPTER 9

"To be a Pilgrim?"

READERS of "Seagull Morning" will recall that the Church and the Chapel were the focal points of many people's lives in Porthleven during my childhood. Porthleven had long enjoyed a reputation for being a religious kind of community, a description which undoubtedly pleased and flattered many people and just as surely annoyed other, less pious members of the public. There was certainly a fair choice of places of worship on offer. In addition to the Parish Church and two large Methodist Chapels there was the Apostolic Church in Thomas' Street (unkindly nicknamed "the Happy Dollies") and the Christadelphian Meeting Room, which in my childhood had occupied premises in The Gue, but later moved to Shute Lane. I understood little about the Christadelphian movement, and cannot pretend, even now, to be particularly well-informed on their beliefs and practices. I noticed, as young people do, the very correct way the ladies dressed to go to service on Sunday afternoons; the fact that most of the men seemed to carry briefcases about with them and, most especially, the fact that they tended - in those days at any rate - to mix with and marry only each other and not to intermingle with the rest of us. I was given to understand, however, that this introversion was in part their great strength: they were reputed to give each other constant help and support, with the consequence that there was about them a comfortable air which one sometimes envied in times of stress.

The Apostolics were quite different: a Pentecostal sect; they believed devoutly in baptism by total immersion and regularly "spoke in tongues." In a society which was much less tolerant of other people's beliefs and practices than most of us affect to be nowadays, this attracted considerable disapproval in some circles, rendering these good people vulnerable to very open and often unkind criticism. Undeterred, they would assemble on the square on summer Saturday evenings, sing hymns to the accompaniment of an ancient harmonium and testify of their beliefs to whoever would listen. One could not but admire their courage.

My parents had opted to send me to a Methodist Sunday School. This was largely because my father, who, it must be admitted, rarely attended a place of worship at all, professed to dislike High Church practice and my mother, though a confirmed Anglican, tended to agree with his point of view. I had therefore grown up in the Methodist tradition, though at the age of thirteen or fourteen I found myself very much drawn to the Church of England. Loyalty was strained. I worked out a system whereby I attended chapel on Sunday mornings and Sunday School in the afternoons, but defected to Evensong at the Parish Church in the evenings. It has to be admitted that my dawning regard for the Established Church was not entirely unconnected with my liking for one of the servers, a boy whose innate blond good looks were enhanced in my eyes by the romantic adornment of cassock and surplice, especially on festival days, when the cassock in question was a red one! This somewhat frivolous diversion ran nonetheless in a sort of double harness with the great pleasure I derived from the service itself. I discovered that, unlike my parents, I loved High Church ritual; delighted in the scent of incense and gloried in the sound of plainsong. I still do!

Despite this attraction I remained, in my way, loyal to Methodism, and at the age of fifteen came into full membership of the church to which I still belong today.

My commitment to the Lord of both church and chapel was to lead me, at the relatively tender age of nineteen, to embark upon an enterprise which, I have to admit, I approached in the most precipitate and ill-considered manner. Our minister at that time was an elderly Welshman named W.O. Luke. Silver-haired and silver-tongued, he was highly popular amongst his congregation. Unfortunately, in the January of 1953 he suffered a serious heart attack and was forbidden to preach for quite some time. The immediate difficulty was the evening service for the following Sunday, to conduct which, it appeared, there was no-one available. Hearing the problem discussed by our elders and betters, I was rash enough to suggest, entirely on the spur of the moment, that perhaps some of us - the young people of the church - could step into the breach and lead worship ourselves that night. Astonishingly enough my offer was accepted, and so it was that I found myself in the pulpit the following Sunday, charged with "doing the address" - it would have been unwise to term it a sermon! In the event, I lasted about five minutes - there must have been many times since when congregations wished I would shut up so promptly, for that occasion proved to be my first step on the way to becoming a fully-fledged Methodist Local Preacher.

It should perhaps be explained, for the benefit of those who are not au fait with the inner workings of the Methodist Church, that it functions on what is known as a

"Circuit" system, whereby one or two ministers are responsible for a group of ten or more churches. They divide their time as best they can, but for obvious reasons great use has to be made of trained lay persons to conduct worship when the ministers are engaged elsewhere. It is deemed, within Methodism, a great privilege to be called to join this august band of helpers.

Looking back, I never wanted to be a preacher. It was something to which I was "led" perhaps against my own better judgment and certainly against my own inclinations. I have never been at all a studious person, but preachers are required to spend a considerable amount of time in study. Particularly in the early days I found the task arduous and demanding. Many were the summer evenings when I should have liked to have been out on the town with my friends, and instead found myself wrestling with the mysteries of 2 Corinthians or comparing Chronicles with Kings and wondering, at times, why I was bothering! It needed all the determination I could muster to quell my own rebelliousness and stick at it "For God's Sake". I am now in a position to assert, however, that the rewards of being a preacher far outweigh the problems of the job, and I think it fair to say that leading worship has probably been the greatest privilege of my life.

Methodist Preachers go through a fairly rigorous training programme in order to equip themselves for the task in hand. However, this is not, of itself, sufficient to make one wise in every respect, and I freely admit to having made some huge blunders in the early stages of my preaching career. One of the most hilarious was when I was taking a service at Breage. I had been told that a young female member of the congregation there had broken her leg playing hockey and was in hospital. I duly mentioned the fact in the prayers of intercession. A few giggles were heard, and when I turned round at the end of the prayer the young woman in question was sitting behind me in the choir! My own sense of humour came to my rescue: boldly I declared how delighted we all were that Pauline had made such a swift recovery. The joke saved the day and the service proceeded.

There was another famous occasion, again very early in my preaching career, when a group of four of us were sent out to lead worship in another of the country chapels. The organist, a lady of mature years, greeted us in the vestry with a long, disappointed face and exclaimed "Aw! You're the Mission Band! I thought we was goin' to 'ave four young men! She was the only person who ever commented adversely on our gender, though she probably reflected the view still held by a good many people, that men make better preachers than women. Perhaps they do - certainly they have the advantage of deeper voices and in consequence can avoid the trap of twittering in the pulpit. I have to say, however, that I received nothing but encouragement and kindness from the men in my congregations - a contributory factor in my never becoming a feminist. There was no need.

The impact of Methodism on the life of Cornwall has been amply documented elsewhere, and needs little comment in these pages. It remains, however, one of the great social phenomena of the history of South West England that the preaching of a fastidious Oxford Don should have such a dramatic effect upon the lives of smugglers, wreckers and hard-bitten tin miners - some of my own ancestors amongst them. The heart of the matter is that Wesley took the Gospel of Jesus Christ out to the people, and they responded. "The Lions of Breage" he wrote in his diary "Are become lambs". It is difficult, at this space of time, to be precisely sure what he meant by that phrase; certainly not that his numerous converts had suddenly become pale shadows of their former selves, with repressed and constricted personalities. The transformation, borne out by Wesley's own writings, seems quite clearly to have related to re-defined characters, arising from people's clear consciousness of being "born again", forgiven by God for past wrongs and enabled by the Holy Spirit to live a renewed life which was vigorously holy. Holiness, erroneously viewed by many of its critics today as equating either to repression or to hypocrisy, might well have signified "wholeness" to the early Methodists, and the quest for it has continued to define Methodism for over two centuries. Certainly the Methodists I knew in my childhood and early youth were a zestful body of people, who appeared to me not merely dedicated to the pursuit of the holy life, but energised and delighted by it. The zealous and enthusiastic singing, for instance, which still tends to mark Methodist worship, is an excellent example of this joyful and outgoing approach to religion and one of the more commendable aspects of the church to which I belonged and belong.

I was one of only three "lady" preachers in those days. The other two were both a great deal older than I was. The senior of the two was Miss Williams, a sweet, gentle lady of uncertain age who was usually referred to as "Ludo". I never fathomed the reason for this soubriquet, but it seemed to suit her. Daisy Stears was much younger than Ludo, but cast very much in the same mould. A passionate Biblical fundamentalist, she always remained equivocal about the role of women in the church, but I remember her saying on one occasion "God raises up women when men fail!" Presumably this helped her to justify her own position when conducting worship. Daisy was a kind and knowledgeable woman and is remembered with affection by those who knew her. I should have liked to have been half as good as she was.

However, I was still very young and shared the foibles of the young, especially where fashion was concerned. Because of this, I came under heavy fire from a particularly prim spinster lady member of one of the country chapels, who had seen me out and about wearing a pair of tartan trews, a prized addition to my wardrobe and the envy of many of my contemporaries. Miss X complained to the minister that "That Miss Giles goes around in men's clothing, contrary to the teachings of St. Paul". My rejoinder to this broadside was that no self-respecting man would be seen in my tartan trews and furthermore, if Miss X could produce any evidence that St. Paul ever wore trousers at all, I would abandon mine forthwith. This elicited a huge guffaw from the Minister and I heard no more of the matter, though Miss X, whilst always scrupulously polite, remained wary of me to the end of her days.

The doyen of the local preachers in those days was a larger-than-life character named James Varcoe Geach. He had been preaching since 1899, and seemed to me to be very old, although at that time he was probably in his early to mid-seventies, and was still extremely active. His shock of iron-grey hair and piercing blue eyes tended to give him the appearance of a latter-day John the Baptist, a role endorsed by his somewhat florid style of preaching. Revered by some and reviled by others, he was a man you could not help noticing. By trade he was a wheelwright and undertaker, though by the time I knew him there was obviously a much reduced demand for the former. He had made his own coffin, and was reputed to sit in it whilst reading the morning papers - a fact which I cannot verify, but it does seem somehow typical of his eccentricity. By the time he was carried to chapel in that coffin he was well over ninety. I attended his funeral and the overflow congregation packed even the chapel yard to capacity.

Mr. Geach was a well-known personality outside the church as well as within it. He enjoyed a reputation for being "long-headed" (a colloquialism for "clever") and was in considerable demand as an unpaid tax consultant. He was also a member of the Kerrier Rural District Council and rose to be its Chairman. In his year of office, however, he required the date of the Kerrier Annual Dinner to be changed because it clashed with the Local Preachers' Meeting, an event he never allowed himself to miss.

The electric lighting in the schoolroom at Sithney had been installed by Mr. Geach in memory of his late wife, a lady to whom he was said to have been engaged for no less than fourteen cautious years before meeting her at the altar. Sadly they had no children and I sometimes thought that J.V. was a rather lonely man, although if that was the case he compensated himself very well with his community and church activities, both round the Circuit and in the chapel at Sithney, where he worshipped regularly.

Sithney, I recall, was a chapel well-endowed with characters. One such was Tom Treloar, a delightful old gentleman who was a gifted musician. He played a number of woodwind instruments, and was especially proficient on the oboe and the clarinet, giving lessons to local would-be experts. He had formed a small woodwind band, which assisted with the music at Sithney chapel, lending it considerable style, especially when Clifford Mollard brought his violin along as well.

Sithney was the scene of one of the most hilarious incidents of my early preaching career. The occasion was a wet, wild evening in early spring. The chapel was not well-filled, to say the least, and this was hardly surprising. We began, as usual, with a hymn, followed by prayers and then another hymn. During the final bars of the last verse, the door opened, and in came a regular member of the congregation, well-known for his idiosyncrasies. On this particular evening, he was wearing yellow oilskins, a motor-cyclist's helmet and heavy boots. He clanked up the aisle to a front pew and having waited for him to be seated I commenced reading the first lesson. However, he then began to divest himself of the oilskins, which crackled loudly. The trousers became stuck over the boots and had to be turned inside out in order to be pulled off. The top had to be pulled over the wearer's head, and on several occasions during this performance, he found it necessary to stand up. Nothing loath, I ploughed on with the Old Testament lesson, whilst the congregation collapsed in silent laughter around me, and it was all I could do not to join in.

Sithney, alas, is no more. Both the chapel and the schoolroom are now private dwellings and the Methodists of Sithney parish worship at combined premises in Breage, named, somewhat prosaically "Breaney".

Rinsey Chapel, also long since closed, was the scene of another comical incident, involving, on this occasion, the members of Porthleven Methodist Youth Club, who at that time ran a preaching team and visited various country chapels to take services. At Rinsey that evening the congregation was minimal and was greatly exceeded by the number of people participating. One young man, who had been allocated the somewhat lowly task of reading the notices, determined to make an impact on the few rather sleepy old people who sat in front of him, and elongated his contribution to the service by making a forceful appeal for support for some event taking place during the coming week. He finally finished and sat down, whereupon an old man in the back pew piped up "They was last week's notices, my son". The entire Youth Club were reduced to helpless laughter at the expense of the hapless member, who nonetheless had the good grace to laugh himself.

Porthleven Methodist Youth Club deserves particular mention in these pages, for it was a considerable force amongst young people in the village at that time. The bulk of its membership was of course drawn from the chapels, though any young person between the ages of fourteen and twenty-one years could join. You did not have to be a Methodist: indeed many young Anglicans, in particular, numbered amongst our membership, and we had some marvellous times together. At its zenith, the club was open three nights a week. Mondays and Thursdays provided the usual games facilities, but Tuesday night was "club night" when a different activity took place each week. This might be a party; or a talk or a demonstration, or competitions or a film or slide show. Amongst these latter a great favourite was "Frank Strike's Wrecks". Frank, a local businessman and Councillor and erstwhile Mayor of Helston had devotedly built up a huge collection of slides of wrecks around our part of the coast: they seemed to hold a grim fascination for the Youth Club boys, who were always rather better behaved on Frank's night than they sometimes were on others.

At Christmas time, we would go out carol singing to the sick and aged in their homes, and there were many amusing incidents during the course of these excursions. On one occasion we visited a house where the old Porthleven phrase "a cup of tea in a basin" was actually illustrated before our eyes. The elderly son of the ancient lady we were visiting sat at the kitchen table throughout the proceedings, his elbows on the oilcloth cover, drinking tea somewhat noisily from a large basin. It was difficult, in the circumstances, to keep a straight face throughout "Silent Night". Somehow we managed. Afterwards, he thanked us briefly for singing to his mother, and resumed his tea-drinking activities.

One of our favourite people to visit was a man called Simon Rule. Simon, who was by then very old, was a well-known character in the district, both as a Methodist Local Preacher and as an entertainer. Diminutive of stature, he stood at about 4 ft 9 ins. He was a natural

156

clown with an inexhaustible fund of funny stories and was consequently much in demand throughout his lifetime as a compère of concerts, his running patter of amusing tales never failing to keep the audience amused between acts - indeed, if the said acts were sufficiently weak, Simon would emerge as the star of the show himself. He was also very keen on cricket: I am told he eventually fulfilled a lifetime's ambition to "stand at the wicket at Lord's". The wicket - there or indeed anywhere else - would have come well up to his waist!

The last time we visited Simon he was extremely frail - we found him looking rather lost in a huge armchair in his sitting room, with a blanket over him, even though there was a roaring fire going in the grate nearby. The ensuing conversation went something like this:-

Roy (our Youth Club Leader): Well Mr. Rule, how are you?

Simon: Not too good, boy. Not too good.

Roy: Sorry to hear that. Perhaps you ought to have stayed in bed today.

Simon: (With a twinkle) No, boy. Missus said to me "Stay in the bed Simon" but I said "No my dear - more die in the bed than out of it - I'll get up".

This was typical of the man. He continued to "get up" for as long as he could, and was mourned by the entire village when he finally passed away later the next year. He was one of our great characters, of whom it can genuinely be said that he was much loved by all who knew him. His infectious laughter, once heard, echoes in the mind for ever. Such people are the more delightful for being rare.

In the New Year, the Youth Club always organised a coach to go to Plymouth for the pantomime. I have never much cared for pantomime, but one would no more have thought of missing this outing than of missing one's own wedding day. It was a ritual. We left the village at some unseemly early hour "to catch the ferry" and we always chose a day when Argyle were playing at home, so that the boys could go to the match whilst the girls frittered away their money in the stores. We usually lunched at a restaurant called "The Magnet" - which cannot have been a very memorable establishment, since I have no recollection at all of anything I ever ate there. If you were feeling rich you dined at Dingle's restaurant, with its magnificent views out over the city; certainly we usually went there for tea, and made use of their facilities to wash and brush up before going to the theatre.

The journey home was even more tedious than the journey up. It was usually made even longer by the fact that there was always someone who was hungry and wanted to stop in Bodmin for fish and chips. We would arrive back in Porthleven in the early hours, exhausted and I suppose to some extent happy. Woe betide us, however, if we failed to turn up for morning service that day - there were always those who seemed to perceive this most innocuous of outings as a licentious piece of debauchery, and to castigate us accordingly.

One Easter time, I think in 1953, we were invited to the village of Ponsangath to give a "sacred" concert on Good Friday evening. Transport would be supplied: there was no need to hire a coach. We duly assembled on the square at about 6 pm on a cold, blustery March evening. The promised transport duly arrived. It was a large cattle truck, scrubbed out and fitted with straw bales for seating, and having a tarpaulin roof, in which was a sizeable hole. This made for a draughty journey, since the wind was keen, and we grew colder and colder as the truck rattled and bumped its way across Goonhilly Downs. Worse was to follow, though the concert itself went well and we were given an excellent supper by the Ponsangath ladies. During that time, however, it had begun to rain, and the discomfort of the cattle truck was compounded by rainwater blowing in through the hole in the roof. We solved the problem in an ingenious and rather unkind way. Michael (he who had once been my Flora Day partner) was home on leave from the RAF, and had chosen to accompany us that evening, probably for lack of anything better to do. He had grown, over the years, very tall. I do not know quite how we persuaded him to do it, but he ended up standing in the middle of the truck with his blond head in the tarpaulin hole, keeping the rest of us snug and dry whilst he got a soaking. Inevitably, the comparison with the boy-who-kept-the-dyke springs to mind, though Michael was in no danger of drowning, and it was almost certainly bravado rather than altruism which led him to act as he did. His gesture, however, was much appreciated.

The Youth Club continued to flourish over a long period of years, a fact due in no small measure to the truly amazing dedication of Roy Kitchen, our club leader, and his wife, Marjorie, to whom I pay unreserved tribute. Roy and Marjorie kept open house for the young people, not just of the church, but of the village. They gave up their time, including their own summer holidays, to take club members on trips abroad, including, memorably, one rather splendid jaunt to Switzerland which was slightly marred when the homeward journey ran into a few minor disasters and took thirty five hours to accomplish! Youth Club served, not only to "keep young people off the streets" but seemed to create a large, jolly, extended family to which all manner of young people belonged and in which they had roles to play. At one point we had, to the best of my recollection, eighty eight members, not all of them particularly easy to deal with, though some of the most difficult were among the most lovable. I became in due course an assistant leader, which meant that sometimes I was left in sole charge of a crowd of teenagers not a great deal younger than I was myself. I can honestly say that, apart from the odd small incident, they gave me no trouble, whilst vandalism - other than the occasional stray dart thrown into the screen at the rear of the Sunday School hall - was non-existent.

I had more trouble with my first Sunday School class than I ever did with the Youth Club. At the tender age of fifteen I had been pressed into service to "teach" a class of rowdy eleven-year-old boys. Little actual teaching took place, as I struggled to keep the group in some sort of order. At any given time there was at least one well-known local troublemaker: when he moved up to the next group, another would replace him. After three years I admitted defeat and asked to be transferred to a class of girls. I found these easier and we actually did manage to work usefully together. It was many years before I ever attempted to teach boys again - much more successfully, then, than the first time round, though it should be noted that one member of my very first class went on to be a highly acceptable Local Preacher - due more, I suspect, to the fact that he came from a very supportive Christian family than to any influence I may have had over him.

There were, at that time, two Methodist Churches in Porthleven. Each one maintained two sizeable buildings, one for Sunday worship and another for Sunday School and all the social occasions during the week. These were many and varied. Women's meetings; Guild evenings; Choir practices; Youth Club; Faith teas; Concerts with suppers to follow; Missionary evenings; Leaders' meetings, Trustees' meetings and many more ensured that the ancillary buildings were used far more than the chapels themselves. The chapels stood aloof, opening their doors for weddings and funerals and Sunday services. They were kept in pristine condition as befitted holy places, and there was considerable rivalry (some of it less than seemly) between the two congregations to ensure high standards. The chapel which I attended, in

Fore Street, has become a Grade Two star listed building and its facade is a small masterpiece of Victorian architecture, though the rear was kept very plain and gave rise to the following jibe:-

"They built the church, upon my word, as fine as any abbey

And then they thought to cheat the Lord, and built the back part shabby".

When I was eighteen, they renovated our chapel. It was a major undertaking for which a great deal of money needed to be raised. In that connection there is a delightful, if apocryphal story of one of our church members who was both very wealthy and notoriously tight-fisted. It is said that, having donated fifty pounds to the renovation fund, he went into the building to inspect the work in its early stages. At that point of time there were workmen on the scaffolding, making repairs to the vaulted ceiling; one of them, accidentally or deliberately, dropped a small lump of plaster on the visitor's head, which he construed as a sign from heaven, and increased his donation to a hundred pounds. I cannot, of course, vouch for the veracity of this tale, but there is probably a grain of truth in it somewhere, and the renovation fund benefited accordingly.

All through the spring of that year the work went on. As March gave way to April the actual decorating was put in hand. The interior walls, which had been painted in a rather cold shade of green for as long as most people could remember, took on the colour of Cornish clotted cream, against which the newly varnished pews glowed warmly. The ancient, faded red soft furnishings were replaced by magnificent new blue velvet ones, the "IHS" on the pulpit fall picked out in gold thread.

This same colour scheme (freshened up from time to time) largely obtains today, though it is interesting to note that some of the seat cushions were never changed, and the old dark red ones are still to be found here and there, nearly fifty years later!

The re-opening of the newly re-furbished chapel was scheduled for the 17th May, the occasion of the sixty-ninth anniversary of that particular building. It was the archetypal Great Village Event, and was talked about for weeks, even months beforehand, with massive planning to ensure that everything would go smoothly on the great day. The programme was ambitious, to say the least. We should begin with a sit-down lunch in the Public Hall, followed by a Procession of Witness to the chapel for the actual re-dedication service, after which the congregation would return to the Public Hall for tea, thus enabling visitors from afar to be adequately fed and watered before assembling back at the chapel in the evening for a performance of Handel's "Messiah" by the (admittedly augmented) choir. My own role in these proceedings was the somewhat minor one of helping to clear tables and wash dishes. Nevertheless, I was greatly looking forward to the whole thing, which promised to be quite an occasion!

The best laid schemes of mice and men, we are told "aft gang agley". So it was in my case. About a fortnight before the re-opening, I fell ill with what proved to be an exceptionally severe bout of "real flu" - something I had never had in my entire life previously, and have only experienced twice since. Fellow-sufferers from this complaint will confirm that it is as far removed from the common cold as the east is from the west, even though some of the symptoms are vaguely similar. I was ordered to bed and was glad to stay there - a most unusual state of affairs. For days on end my limbs ached abominably: I was feverish, with the worst pain in the head that I have ever experienced. For days I sipped drinks of water and ate virtually nothing. Flora Day came and went: utterly debilitated and demoralised by then, I celebrated it by getting dressed for the first time and creeping downstairs to sit miserably hunched over the fire, for the day was chilly. To add to my misery Peter, my pet canary, died - he had been a present from my father for my eighth birthday and had therefore sung for me for ten long years. Now his song was silenced. Wallowing in self-pity I wept copious tears whilst my mother dug a small grave under the hydrangea bush and laid him to rest.

Despite all this, I was determined not to miss the chapel re-opening, and made strenuous efforts to get fit over the next week. My attempted fast recovery was not assisted when, the first time I appeared in public, I was told by a tactless acquaintance that I looked "Like a woman who has just had a very bad confinement!" This somewhat discouraging comment served only to strengthen my resolution, and on the great day, still feeling well below par, I presented myself for duty at the Public Hall wearing what, with hindsight, was probably a somewhat unwise choice of dress - red, with a pattern of large blue and yellow flowers. I suppose it had at least the merit of being cheerful, though it probably served to emphasise the fact that my complexion still resembled uncooked pastry after the ravages of the 'flu.

The chaos in the Public Hall that morning had to be experienced to be believed, and the memory of it has never left me. Hosts of middle-aged ladies, most of them apparently suffering the discomfort of menopausal hot flushes, dashed about with pinafores over their best clothes, carving hams and chickens, preparing salads, and frantically laying three enormously long tables, with a fourth "top" table reserved for the visiting dignitaries. Fortunately, Porthleven Public Hall is a fairly large building; every place for lunch was taken. I have to say that it all looked beautiful; the white napery; the gleaming cutlery; people's best dinner plates, lovingly loaned for this great occasion, and the glittering glassware, the contents of which were, of course, strictly non-alcoholic!

The meal was followed, as such meals usually are, by a round of predictably dull speeches and polite applause, whilst we fidgeted in the background, anxious to begin clearing the tables so they could be re-laid for tea. Any hopes we had entertained of joining the procession and attending the service were quickly dispelled. I have never in my life seen so many dirty dishes piled up in one small space. All that afternoon we wrestled with those dishes. One of the younger ladies, Opre Griffin, became so frustrated that she filled a large bath with unwashed plates and commandeered a couple of male helpers to carry it to her house, where at least she would have unfettered use of a sink, the Public Hall in those days boasting only one - somewhat inadequate for the task in hand. Sorting out the washed plates and returning them to their owners was an exercise in itself; somehow it was accomplished, as these things always are in villages. Occasionally, the walls seemed to sway towards me: determined not to give in to my convalescent state and go home, I soldiered on with the rest, and between us we ensured that the tea tables were daintily laid on time - just.

Was I, someone enquired, going to hear the "Messiah" in the evening? No, I was not. My post-invalid self could not contemplate a further two hours in a crowded building. Instead, I opted to go for a short walk on my own. The evening was cool and still - a welcome respite after the frenzied stuffiness of the swarming Public Hall. I walked slowly round Green Lane, a favourite route of mine, and sniffed the sweet scents of the May evening. Passing the chapel on my way home, however, I stopped outside to listen. It was an amazing moment, and a total contrast to everything that had gone before in that "commotious" and stressful day. The choir were singing "And the Glory of the Lord". It was a sound to bring a lump to the throat and tears to the eyes. I stood there in the empty street, looking down towards the harbour. Our village was still; the music poured out of the building like a benediction upon it. Strange feelings floated somewhere at the back of my brain - feelings which I have only now come to try to put into words. The Glory of the Lord? Here? In Porthleven? In this irritating, outspoken, quarrelsome, difficult Cornish village? In this chaotic, muddly little society with its continual storms in teacups and its in-fighting over things that matter very little anyway? The Glory of the Lord? In this hotbed of gossip and interference in other people's affairs? In this unimportant, inconsequential, insignificant little place? Is such a thing possible? The music swelled to its climax. I looked at our village, which I loved, and still love. "The Glory of the Lord shall be revealed". Here? In Porthleven? Yes, a glimpse, maybe. Just maybe.

EPILOGUE

And Tomorrow . . . .

AND so, after my fashion, I grew up, if anyone can ever be said to have done so, since true maturity seems, for most of us, to be well-nigh impossible to attain. My own reluctance to grasp the nettle of adulthood was based upon a premise that once you finished growing up you began to grow old, and though I have since discovered that for the latter condition there is no known remedy, I still believe that vigorous resistance to it can be nothing but healthy. Nonetheless, time and experience inevitably change us all, however much we may try to defy the process. Perhaps Porthleven and I have grown old together! I am now none of the people I describe myself as being in the pages of this book, and cannot judge whether that is a good or a bad thing. In much the same way, Porthleven is no longer the place it used to be. It was a village: now we call it a town, and it has acquired both the advantages and the problems of being one. Happily, much of the innate zest and exuberance for which it was always famous remain, albeit somewhat obscured by a questionable veneer of modern sophistication. It has always been a place with a strong sense of its own identity and hopefully always will be. But there was a time, sadly gone for ever, when you could walk down Fore Street and, give or take the odd summer visitor, you would know by name everyone you met; you would greet them and they would greet you. Now, although the old courtesies are still observed by some of us, we speak to strangers, whose names we do not know, and whose histories are a closed book to us, as ours are to them. Perhaps what I have recorded in this volume will serve to illuminate, however dimly, a past well-remembered by those who shared it, which is precious in our minds and, for better or worse, made us what we are.

Memory, however, is not a bath in which to wallow: it is a stage upon which today's drama is played out. It is good to remember - but it is better to look forward. One mourns the passing of innocence, but without its loss there can be no acquisition of true wisdom. We cannot stand for ever under a cherry tree in the May sunlight. The tree itself changes, and its autumnal glory can be every bit as beautiful as its spring splendour. Being young was wonderful, but I would not go back, even if I could.

"This is the state of man - today he puts forth the tender leaves of hope - tomorrow blossoms....."

But that, as they say, is another story.